American Manners and Customs-2

A Second Guide for Newcomers

More
of the
Best of
Easy English
NEWS

Elizabeth Claire

Eardley Publications

Photos from Bigstockphoto.com

Developmental Editors: Kelly Cunningham, Samantha Coles, Ann Early,
Marilyn Gelman
Copy Editors: Adelaide Coles, Jeanne Trabulsi, Nadine Simms
Design: Steve Jorgensen
Cover Design: Elizabeth Claire

©2018 Eardley Publications
Virginia Beach, VA 23456

Printed in the United States of America

0 1

ISBN: 978-0-937630-20-4

This book is dedicated to you,
the Newcomer

Welcome!

Dear Newcomers,

Many of you have told me how valuable *American Manners and Customs-1* has been for you. You told me that it saved you many embarrassing moments, helped you make friends, and helped you understand Americans better.

You've been asking for more, so here is more. Twenty articles in this second book about American manners and customs are taken from past issues of *Easy English NEWS*. I've added to them and completely updated them to today's changing customs and manners. Thank you for asking me to write it.

Elizabeth Claire

Since *American Manners and Customs Book One*, my newspaper, *Easy English NEWS* has won the prestigious Intellectual Contribution to Society award from Mensa's Educational and Research Foundation.

Here's a bit about me: I graduated *magna cum laude* and received my B.A. in Spanish and Education from the City College of New York. I received my Master's Degree in Teaching English as a Second Language from New York University on an Experienced Teacher Fellowship. I've taught English as a second language to students of all ages from many countries and have trained teachers in the United States, Japan, and the Czech Republic. With Mariko Sasaki, we founded *Easy English NEWS* to help newcomers understand their new environment and culture and to feel welcome here. *Easy English NEWS* has been serving ESL classes and individuals since 1996.

My other books for English language learners and teachers are available at **www.elizabethclaire.com**
:

American Manners and Customs-1 ESL Teacher's Activities Kit
ESL Holiday Activities Kit
Classroom Teacher's ESL Survival Kit #1 (with Judie Haynes)
Classroom Teacher's ESL Survival Kit #2 (with Judie Haynes)
Dangerous English for a Dangerous World
Easy English Crossword Puzzles
ESL Phonics For All Ages: A Series of Six Books Plus Audio CDs
ESL Wonder Workbook #1: This Is Me
ESL Wonder Workbook #2: All Around Me
Just-A-Minute!
Kristina, 1904: The Greenhorn Girl
The New Boy Is Lost! With Audio CD, and Teacher's Guide and Activity Book
Three Little Words: A, An, and The
CD: Easy Songs for English Language Learners
On Kindle:
What's So Funny?
Voices of Our New Neighbors Volumes 1, 2, 3

Contents

1. Birthdays 6

2. Special Ages 10

3. Birth Signs and Birthstones 14

4. Schools in the United States 18

5. Tips for Success in School 22

6. Bullying in Schools 26

7. High School Graduation 30

8. Higher Education 34

9. Paying for College 38

10. Friendship in the United States 42

11. Gender in the United States 46

12. Love and Romance 50

13. Getting Engaged 54

14. A Traditional Wedding 58

15. A Wedding Guest 62

16. Having a Baby in the United States 66

17. Other Ways to Become Parents 70

18. Taking Care of Children in the United States 74

19. Keeping Children Safe 78

20. Family Pets 82

Answers to Quizzes 86

Word Help / Glossary 89

1. Birthdays

How old are you?

Be careful when you ask this question. It's a polite question if you are asking a child, teenager, or young adult. Older people might think it's **rude*** if you ask them how old they are. Many women never tell their age.

However, most people over 80 will gladly tell you. They are glad they have lived so long. A pleasant thing to say to them is "Wow, you don't look it!"

When does a person's age begin?

Americans and most Europeans and South Americans start a person's age from the day they were born. They add one year to their age on their birthday.

 In some Asian countries, people say that a baby is a year old when it is born. (They count the time that the child has been alive inside the mother as the first year.) In addition, in some Asian countries, people become a year older on New Year's Day.

This difference **creates*** problems when Asian children come to an American school.

For example, two children, an American and a Korean, both enter a new school in January 2017. Both children were born in December 2002. "How old are you?" asks the school **secretary***. Even though they were born in the same month in the same year, the American says, "I'm 14." The Korean says, "I'm 16."

Some South Americans celebrate their saint's day*, not their own birthday. They might not know when their birthdays are.

Birthday Customs

There are many customs for birthdays in the United States.

American parents want their children to feel special on this day. The "birthday child" may choose the food for dinner. The family may have a party. Parents and friends give gifts to the birthday child.

There is an old custom of a birthday "**spanking***." A parent gives the child a gentle spanking. They give one spank on the birthday child's **buttocks*** for each year, and one extra spank. Or it might be gentle punches on the upper arm. Then the child is supposed to have a year of good luck. It's not OK for others to do this.

The birthday cake

A birthday cake with candles is an important part of the celebration. For a young person, there is one candle for each year, plus one extra candle in the middle "to grow on." On an older person's cake, there may be just one candle or a candle for each ten years. Everyone sits or stands around the

birthday person. Someone lights the candles on the cake. Someone turns off the lights. People start to sing "Happy Birthday" as they bring the cake to the table. They set the cake with its burning candles in front of the birthday person.

The birthday person thinks of a wish. She must not tell the wish to anyone. Then she tries to blow out all of the candles. People say that, "If you can blow out all of the candles at once, the wish will come true." The birthday person cuts the first piece of cake and serves it.

Birthdays at school

Elementary schools may have birthday customs for children. On a birthday, a child may bring a small **treat*** for everyone in the class. (Schools may have a **guide*** for treats. This is because many children have become overweight from eating too many **sweets***. Many children have **allergies***. Some schools say *no sweets*. Others say, *no cupcakes, no* **gluten***, *no peanuts, no home-made* **snacks***.) At some schools, children may give out pencils, stickers, or some other **non-edible*** treat. The class may sing *Happy Birthday* to the birthday child.

Older people's birthdays

Many older people do not **make a fuss over*** their birthdays. They may have dinner or cake with family. Close friends may send birthday greetings by email, on Facebook, or mail a birthday card.

An office, store, factory, or other workplace may have its own birthday customs. There may be a birthday card for everyone to sign with birthday wishes. They may write things such as *Happy birthday, and many more! Love from [or* **Sincerely*,***] Maria Rivera)*. In some workplaces, someone may collect a few dollars from each worker to get a gift for the birthday person.

The years 21, and the years ending in zero (30, 40, 50, etc.) are a little more special. Family or friends may make a party. A man's friends may send cards making fun of "how old" he is now. Some cards may make a joke about the number of candles on the cake. Birthday cards for older women are more

often **complimentary***: "Still looking good!" If you don't know a person well, choose a friendly card!

Surprise parties

Sometimes a friend or family member will make a surprise party for a person's birthday. They tell **guests*** to keep it a secret. Guests must not tell the birthday person about the surprise. The guests must arrive at the party early, before the birthday person.

To make sure the birthday person comes to the place of the party, a friend makes up a story: "Come see the new curtains I bought," or "Could you help me?" When the birthday person walks in the door, everyone yells "Surprise!"

Let's talk about it.

1. At what event do Americans start counting a person's age? When do they add a year to their age? Is this different from the custom in your home country?

2. Tell four traditions for American birthdays.

3. What are some traditions in your home country for birthdays?

4. When is your birthday? How do you celebrate it?

5. How do people prepare for a surprise party for a friend or family member?

6. Have you ever been to a surprise party for someone? Tell about it.

Using new words:
Match the word with its meaning.

_____ 7. to say something to show admiration

_____ 8. a small meal

_____ 9. a person who is invited to someone's home or a party

_____ 10. to pay a lot of attention to something or do special things for something

_____ 11. not polite

A. rude

B. snack

C. make a fuss over

D. compliment

E. guest

Write a word in each sentence to make it correct. Choose from this list:
saint   yell   spanking   secret   candles

12. Some parents give a child a gentle _____ on his or her birthday.

13. At a surprise party, the guests may _____ "Surprise!" when the birthday person arrives.

14. Don't tell anyone about the party. Keep it a _____.

15. South Americans may celebrate their birthday on their _____'s day.

16. A birthday person's "wish will come true" if he or she blows out all of the _____ on the birthday cake.

2. Special Ages

Certain ages have special meanings in the United States.

Babies from **newborn*** to one year old are called *infants*. When they begin to walk, they are called *toddlers*. In most states,  children must start **kindergarten*** or first grade by age six. Many children go to nursery school, preschool, or **Headstart*** at age three or four. State laws also tell the age that a child no longer needs to go to school. In most states, students may not leave school before the age of 16.

Children aged 10 to 11 are ***pre-teens****. Children aged 12 to 18 are called ***adolescents****. Ages 13 to 19 are *teens*. People in their 20s are *young adults*.

 Depending on the state, 15- or 16-year-olds may get a **permit*** to learn to drive a car.

 The 16th birthday is an important time. A girl may have a special birthday party called a "Sweet Sixteen Party."

Laws in most states say that parents must **support*** their children until the age of 18. Some parents support their children for many years after that, too.

 At 18, young people may live **on their own***. They are allowed to work at any kind of job. (People younger than 18 may not do dangerous kinds of work.)

 At 18, people may sign **contracts.*** An 18-year-old citizen may vote. An 18-year old does not need a parent's **consent*** to get married. *With* parents' consent, the age for marriage is different in different states. Most states use the age of 16 for both boys and girls. In seven states, girls may get married at the age of 15 if they have their parent's consent.

Laws about sex are different and quite **complicated*** in each state. In many states, a person over 18 who has sex with a person under age 18 is **committing* rape***. It doesn't matter that the younger person agreed to the sex. The *age of consent* is the age (by law) that a person is responsible for decisions about sex. This is different in different states. In some states, it is 14. The **federal*** age of consent is 12.

At 18, young men and women may join the **Armed Services*** if they choose to. In any case, ALL young men between 18 and 25 must **register*** with **Selective Service***. This doesn't mean they will be **drafted*.** The list for Selective Service is in case of a national **emergency***. Women do not have to register.

Twenty-one is the **legal drinking age*** in most states.

A **representative*** to Congress must be at least 25 years old. Most are over 35. A U.S. **senator*** must be at least 30 years old. The President of the United States must be at least age 35. The youngest president of the U.S. was Theodore Roosevelt. He was 42 when he became president.

Middle age is not a popular term. No one agrees when it begins. Some say it's the years between 35 and 60. Others say it is between the time that one's children leave home and the year of **retirement***. At any rate, our idea of *middle age* gets older each year!

The "Big Four-O" (a 40th birthday) is a time of jokes about getting old. Friends may tease a 40-year-old person. They say that age 40 is the beginning of "the Great Downhill Slide." On the other hand, they may say that "It's **nifty*** to be fifty." Or, "Sixty is the new forty."

Retirement

The years after a person retires from work are often called "the Golden Years." People retire at various ages. It depends partly on the income they will have if they are not working. Americans who have paid into the **Social Security system*** for ten or more years can collect a **pension*** when they retire. At age 67, for people born in and after 1960, a person can collect the full pension. However, some people choose to take early retirement starting at age 62.

The early pension will be smaller. Social Security is usually not enough income to live on. Some business companies **contribute*** to pension plans for their workers, as well. Many Americans have not saved enough for retirement. They may work at part time jobs.

When is someone "old"?

The answer **depends*** on who you ask. A child may think someone aged 50 is old. A 50-year-old person may think that someone is old at age 80. People in their 80s and 90s say, "You're only as old as you feel." It's more polite to say "an **elderly*** gentleman/woman" than to say, "an old man/ woman."

Americans use the term *senior citizen** for older people. Senior Centers have activities for older people. Many stores, theaters, and buses have **discount*** prices for senior citizens. (The lower prices may be at certain times or on certain days.)

Octogenarians* are people in their 80s. *Nonagenarians** are in their nineties, and *centenarians** are 100 years or older.

Anniversaries*

The tenth, twenty-fifth, and fiftieth anniversaries are important anniversaries for weddings, businesses, and other events.

The first anniversary is called the "Paper Anniversary." The 25th anniversary is called the "Silver Anniversary." The 50th anniversary is called the "Golden Anniversary." The 75th anniversary is called the "Diamond Anniversary."

Let's talk about it.

1. What are words for people of these ages:

    a. babies under one year?

    b. children starting to walk, up to age 3?

    c. children aged 10 to 12?

    d. children aged 13 to 19?

    e. people in their 20s?

    f. people over 60?

2. In the US, what happens at these ages:

    a. age 6?

    b. age 16?

    c. age 18?

    d. age 21

    e. age 65, 66, or 67

3. What are special ages in your home country? What happens at those ages?

4. What anniversaries are important?

Using new words:

Match the word with its meaning.

_____	5. At what age can a person who was born in 1960 retire with a full Social Security pension?	A. 18
_____	6. An octogenarian is in his or her ____.	B. senior
_____	7. The president must be at least ___ years old.	C. 35
_____	8. The U.S. Armed Services: Army, Navy, Air Force, or Marines are part of the _____.	D. 67
_____	9. An older person is a ____ citizen.	E. 80s
_____	10. A U.S. citizen can vote at age ___.	F. Armed Services

Write a word in each sentence to make it correct. Choose from this list:
anniversary   learner's permit   Selective Service   preschool

11. Before ages 5 or 6, many young children attend _____.

12. In many states, a young person may get a _____ _____ to drive a car at age 15.

13. Young men between 18 and 25 must register with _____ _____.

14. Couples celebrate their silver _____ after 25 years of marriage.

3. Birth Signs* and Birthstones*

3.

Birth Signs* and Birthstones*

The Zodiac*

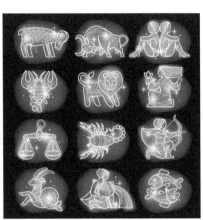

Some Americans think that their birth sign tells something about a person. The birth sign is the **constellation*** behind the sun at the time a person was born. Some people think that it's possible to know a person's **character*** by their birth sign.

There are 12 months of the zodiac. The zodiac is the overhead **path*** in the sky that the sun seems to travel in a year. There are twelve constellations in that path. The constellations in the Zodiac are:

- March 21 to April 20: *Aries* the **Ram***
- April 21 to May 20: *Taurus* the **Bull***
- May 21 to June 20: *Gemini* the **Twins***
- June 21 to July 20: *Cancer* the **Crab***
- July 21 to August 20: *Leo* the Lion
- August 21 to September 20: *Virgo* the **Virgin***
- September 21 to October 20: *Libra* the **Scales***
- October 21 to November 20: *Scorpio* the **Scorpion***
- November 21 to December 20: *Sagittarius* the **Archer***
- December 21 to January 20: *Capricorn* the Goat
- January 21 to February 20: *Aquarius* the Water Carrier
- February 21 to March 20: *Pisces* the Fish

Astrology*

An American may ask a new friend, *What's your birth sign?* That person may say, *I'm Leo.* People look up their own sign or other people's sign to see what **astrologers*** say about such a person.

For example, one astrologer says: *Aries are leaders. They are brave and **energetic***. They love to start things but are not good at finishing things. Aries are very **creative*** but not very neat. They are **frank*** and may hurt people without thinking. They are **loyal*** to their friends and family.*

Some people ask an astrologer to give **advice*** about love, business, health, starting new activities, or taking a vacation.

The astrologer asks for the year, month, hour, and minute a person was born. They want to know the exact place, too. The astrologer uses this information to prepare a **chart***. The chart will show the person's character and events that might happen in the future. Some people pay a lot for an astrological chart. An astrologer may tell a person that the best partner may be a person with a **"sympathetic*** sign."** For example, they may say that an Aries will get along best with another Aries, or a Leo, or a Virgo. And that

a relationship between an Aries and a Scorpio will be **stormy***.

Horoscopes*

Newspapers and the Internet print daily horoscopes for each sign of the zodiac. A horoscope gives **vague*** advice about activities that may be good or bad on this day.

Most Americans think such horoscopes are **silly***. They read them anyway. If planets and stars told our future, then everyone born at the same hour in the same hospital would have the same future. They don't, do they? About 25% of Americans, including some very well-educated people, believe astrology is a true science.

Birthstones and birth flowers

Each month has a **precious stone*** that is lucky for a person born that month. These are called *birthstones*.

Birth months have special flowers, and colors too. According to the American **Gem*** Society, these are the birthstones:

- January's birthstone is a *garnet*. January's flower is the *carnation* or *snowdrop*.

- February's birthstone is an *amethyst*. Its flower is the *violet*.

- March's birthstone is the *aquamarine*. Its flower is the *jonquil*.

- April's birthstone is a *diamond* or *white sapphire*. April's flower is the *daisy* or *sweet pea*.

- May's birthstone is the *emerald*. Its flower is the *lily of the valley*.

- June's birthstone is the *pearl*. Its flower is the *rose*.

- July's birthstone is the *ruby*. Its flowers are the *delphinium, larkspur,* or *water lily*.

- August's birthstone is the *peridot*. Its flowers are *gladiolus* or *poppy*.

- September's birthstone is a *sapphire*. Its flowers are the *aster* or *morning glory*.

- October's birthstone is the *opal* or *tourmaline*. Its flower is the *marigold*.

- November's birthstone is the *yellow topaz*. Its flower is the *chrysanthemum*.

- December's birthstone is the *turquoise*. Its flower is the *daffodil, narcissus,* or *holly*.

For a birthday, a girl's parents (or a sweetheart) might give her a ring, earrings, or other jewelry with her birthstone.

Birthstones		
January		Garnet
February		Amethyst
March		Aquamarine
April		Diamond
May		Emerald
June		Pearl
July		Ruby
August		Peridot
September		Sapphire
October		Opal
November		Topaz
December		Turquoise

Let's talk about it.

1. What is the zodiac?

2. What are the twelve signs of the zodiac?

3. What is your birth sign?

4. What do astrologers say are the characteristics of a person with your birth sign? (Check a book or the Internet for this information.)

5. Does that information describe you well? How are you different from an astrologer's description of a person with your birth sign?

6. Do you think an astrologer could tell anything about a person just from the person's date of birth? How would it be possible?

7. Who is your best friend? What is his or her birth sign?

8. Do people in your home country believe in this kind of astrology? Is there a different system of astrology? Tell about it.

9. What is your birthstone? What is your birth flower?

Using new words:
Match the word with its meaning.

_____ 10. two children who were born together

_____ 11. true to a friend, family, or country

_____ 12. a picture formed by stars in the night sky

_____ 13. information and suggestions about how to do something

_____ 14. a precious stone

_____ 15. a male sheep

_____ 16. daily advice for people based on their birth signs

A. constellation

B. gem

C. ram

D. twins

E. loyal

F. advice

G. horoscope

Write a word in each sentence to make it correct. Choose from this list:
precious   astrology   ambitious   bull

17. A person who works hard to reach high and difficult goals is _____.

18. Diamonds, pearls, and rubies are _____ stones.

19. A _____ is a strong male animal. The female of this animal is a cow.

20. The study of how stars and planets affect a person's character is

_____.

4.

Schools in the United States

Most American children go to free **public*** schools. There are also private schools and **parochial*** schools. There are no *national* **standards*** for schools.

Teachers must have a certificate from the state to teach in a public school. Each town or city **controls*** its own public schools. The **local* Board of Education** makes many decisions about education, students, and teachers. Local taxpayers pay for most of a public school's expenses. State

governments pay a part. The **federal*** government sends money for special programs such as English as a Second Language.

Private schools and parochial schools charge **tuition***. Some of the cost of parochial schools are paid by the church that runs them.

A **principal*** is in charge of the school building, the teachers, and the education of all the students. Large schools may have one or more **vice principals*** as well. There are teachers for regular subjects such as math, English, social studies, foreign languages, and science. There are teachers of music, art, and physical education. Other people in schools are the school nurse; librarian (**media specialist***); **custodians***; and **guidance counselors***. There may be a **remedial**

reading* teacher, speech teacher, and **student teachers***. There may be teacher **aides*** and **paraprofessionals*** in some classes. The school office has **secretaries***. **Crossing guards*** help children cross streets safely on the way to school. The **custodian*** takes care of the school building.

Charter schools*

Some school districts have charter schools. These are public schools that have their own rules. The school day may be longer. Students may have more homework. Parents must **apply*** to send their children to a charter school. There might be a **lottery*** to see who can enter.

Who goes to school?

Public schools must educate all children. That includes children with **disabilities***. Teachers must help children whose **vision*** or hearing is **impaired***, children with **autism***, and children in wheelchairs. There may be aides in the classroom to help these children as well.

Many schools have **ESL*** programs to help **immigrant*** students learn English. In some

schools, a **bilingual*** program helps students learn in their **native language***.

Informal* classrooms

American classrooms are less **formal*** than classrooms in most other countries. Teachers are often friendly. The teacher is not the only **source*** of knowledge in the classroom. Students learn **research skills*** and learn to think for themselves. They learn how to use computers and **calculators***. They don't spend a lot of time time **memorizing*** facts.

Even though the classroom is less formal, there are simple rules to follow. Students should raise their hand when they want to ask a question or make a **comment***. It is **rude*** to talk to a classmate while the teacher is giving a lesson. It **disturbs*** others who want to learn. Students need permission to leave the classroom to go the bathroom. Also, schools have rules against fighting, bullying, and touching.

Technology in school

A classroom may have a "smart board." This is a white board that has a computer in it. A smart board can save anything that the teacher or students write on it. A smart board can connect to the Internet to find information, or show videos on **Youtube.**

Some schools give older students **laptops***, **iPads**, **tablets**, or notebook computers. Students must be careful not to lose or **damage*** these devices. (Parents may have to pay for them.)

The laptops or other devices let students type their homework. They can search for information from the Internet. They

can spell-check their homework. Students can **access*** the school's website to get lessons they missed when they were absent.

Projects*

Teachers often ask students to do projects. The students choose **topics*** to research. They use the school library and the Internet. The students may give a talk to the class to tell what they learned. Students often work in groups. Each member of the group does part of a project. This **cooperative learning*** prepares students for working on a team in business and **industry***.

Report cards*

The school year is divided into **marking periods***. Students' parents get report cards for their children at the end of each marking period. After that, teachers may invite parents to a short **conference***. They talk about their child's **progress***. A parent can ask for a conference at other times, too.

Part of a student's **grade*** is **based on*** classroom **participation***. This can be difficult for students with limited English.

Students usually have one or two hours of homework after school. (High school students have more.) Most American students have time for sports, after-school activities, or a part-time job.

Schools have **drills*** for various emergencies. It's important to follow instructions. Bells ring for fire drills. Students leave the building quietly. There may be practice "lockdowns." Students stay in their classroom quietly. A lockdown is a drill if a shooter comes into the building. (This is not likely, but the drill is important.) In parts of the country there may be earthquake drills or tornado drills.

Let's talk about it.

1. In what ways does each state control its schools?

2. How does the local board of education control public schools?

3. What are some ways the U.S. government controls schools?

4. How do principals and teachers control schools?

5. How do students control schools?

6. How does your ESL class help you?

7. How can parents learn more about or help in their children's schools?

8. What is the purpose of report cards?

9. About how many hours of homework is the right amount for you to do each night? Does your school give more or less homework than school in your home country?

Using new words:
Match the word with its meaning.

_____ 10. Students continue learning in their native language in a _____.

A. marking period

_____ 11. not polite

B. rude

_____ 12. related to a church

C. bilingual program

_____ 13. A person must have a teaching _____ from the state in order to teach in a public school.

D. certificate

E. parochial

_____ 14. Students get a report card at the end of each _____.

F. research

_____ 15. to find material for a project from the Internet, library, books, experts, etc.

Write a word in each sentence to make it correct. Choose from this list:
standards   impaired   research   board   conference

16. The _____ of education in a town hires teachers and sets teacher's salaries.

17. A person who cannot hear well is hearing _____.

18. Students may have to do _____ to complete projects in their classes.

19. Each state sets _____ for schools in that state.

20. Teachers may invite parents to school to have a _____ about a student.

5. Tips* for Success in School

American schools are different. Newcomers must struggle with new subjects, and new teachers and classmates, as well as a new language.

Tips for English language learners

Don't take too many subjects your first years in a U.S. high school or college. Take classes that are **similar*** to classes you've had in your home country. Math, health, art, and music may be easier to learn. American history and English **literature*** classes might be very different from subjects in your home country. They **require*** a lot of reading.

Take care of your health

Eat healthful foods. Exercise. You need extra sleep. English language learners are **constantly*** hearing new words and ideas. Your brain gets tired!

Know what you must know

Find out the **requirements*** of your classes early in the year. Ask the teacher to tell you which **chapters*** of the book you need to read during the year. (Often a teacher **skips*** some chapters.)

Use native-language* books, audio CDs, and videos

Read information in your own language for your subjects. This way, you can understand the facts and **concepts*** in the topic. Then read your textbook to get the English **vocabulary***. Many textbooks have an audio reading **available*** online.

Do you have to read a famous **novel*?** Get the novel in your own language, too. Go to your school's **media center*** or to the public library. Ask if there is a movie or audio CD of the novel. Find out where you can **borrow*** or rent it. This will help you see the place, **characters***, and action in the novel. It can help you get started. However, watching the movie is not a **substitute*** for reading the book.

How to study

Keep a notebook or a part of your notebook for each subject.

Read a chapter *before* the teacher teaches a lesson about it. Write notes about the chapter in your notebook. Then read it again after the lesson. Look at the pictures and read the **captions***. When you read a chapter, notice the **headings***. After you read about a topic, write your notes in a notebook.

Read the chapter and your notes again before a chapter test. **Review*** the textbook. Review your notes before the final exam.

Use your dictionary

Learn the important vocabulary in a chapter. Try to guess the meanings of some words by the rest of the sentence. Carry a **bilingual*** dictionary with you to classes. (An **electronic*** bilingual dictionary is lighter and can be faster.) Write new words and their meanings in your notebook for that subject. Keep your notebook neat, so you can study it easily.

Get a buddy* in the classroom

Some teachers **assign*** a buddy to new students. You can ask for one, too. Ask a friendly classmate for their phone number or email address. You may need to call about the homework if you are absent. Some teachers may post the homework at the school's website. Learn how to get that.

Neatness counts

Practice writing until your handwriting is easy to read and looks good. Learn how to type. Do important **assignments*** on the computer.

Writing tips

When you write a paper, first make a list of ideas. Then write a **rough draft.*** Read it out loud to yourself. This will help you to find your own mistakes. Make all your changes and corrections. If you are using a computer, run **spell check***. Read your paper again to make sure spell check did not enter new errors. Then print it out to hand in to the teacher.

Speak!

Try to **participate*** in class **discussions***. Raise your hand to give an answer or ask for information. Don't worry about making mistakes. Of course you will make mistakes! It's the way to learn.

Sometimes, others will laugh when your words sound funny or you give a wrong answer. Just laugh with them. Ask classmates to help you **pronounce*** words correctly. Teach them to say a short sentence in your language. They'll see that it's difficult.

Talk to the teacher

Ask questions when you don't understand.

Part of your

report-card **grade*** may come from participation. Another part will come from **effort***. How will the teacher know the effort you are putting in? Show it. Show the teacher the vocabulary list of the words that are new for you. Tell the teacher how much time you spend on homework.

Students often work in groups.

If the teacher **offers*** help during lunch or after school, **accept*** it!

Take part in some **extra-curricular activities*** at school. These are a good place to make friends, practice English, and learn other **skills***.

A high school marching band

Many schools have a Back-to-School Night in September. This is a time for parents to visit the school and their child's classroom.

Parents may question teachers about their child's **progress***. They can tell the teacher how the student feels about the class. They can tell about any problems the student has with homework or understanding the lesson. Parents can join a PTA (Parent--Teacher Association). This group talks about school problems. They raise money for special programs or **scholarships***.

Let's talk about it.

1. Is your American classroom different from classrooms in your home country? In what ways?

2. Have you done any projects in school? Tell about one of them.

3. What kind of projects do you like to do?

4. How many subjects are you studying this year? Are they all in English? How much homework do you have for each class?

5. What can you do when the textbook for a subject is difficult to understand?

6. Is it easy or difficult for you to participate in class lessons? Why is it important?

7. How do you feel when someone laughs at the way you pronounce words?

8. What tips for success can you give to a new student?

Using new words:
Match the word with its meaning.

_____ 9. the words under a photograph or picture

_____ 10. a person in a story

_____ 11. a thing or person that takes the place of something else

_____ 12. the first writing of an essay or project, not the final version

_____ 13. novels, stories, poetry

_____ 14. sports, clubs, marching band

_____ 15. A long story

A. substitute

B. novel

C. extra-curricular activities

D. literature

E. caption

F. character

G. rough draft

Write a word in each sentence to make it correct. Choose from this list:
media center   electronic   heading   assignment   requirements

16. An _____ bilingual dictionary can help a person quickly learn the meaning of a word.

17. A _____ tells the reader what the next paragraphs are about.

18. You can do research in the school's _____.

19. Each teacher has _____ for passing a subject.

20. It's important to know the homework _____ each day.

6. Bullying* in Schools

Bullying is a serious problem in some schools. It can happen in any **grade***. Schools try to stop this **behavior***. Sadly, newcomers are often the targets of bullying.

What is bullying?

Bullying is when a stronger person or a group of people hurt a weaker person. There

are many ways that some **unkind*** people bully others:

- They may hit or **threaten*** to hit a person.
- They may **make fun of*** a person's language, skin color, religion, clothes, appearance, **disability***, size, **sexual orientation***, schoolwork, or personality.
- They may **insult*** and call a person bad names.
- They may stop a person from having friends.
- They may take or **damage*** a person's **property***.

What is cyberbullying*?

Cyberbullying is when a person uses **social media*** on the Internet to hurt or **embarrass*** someone. The bully **posts*** information, photos, or lies about a person on **Facebook***, or sends messages on **Twitter***, or sends a person hateful emails. The bully can be **anonymous*** on the Internet. He or she doesn't have to be stronger than a person to hurt a **victim**.

Who bullies?

There is something sad about a person who bullies others. The person may feel that others are better-looking, have better grades, or have more friends than they do. Bullying may cover up their own feelings of **inferiority***. Bullying makes them feel special and important.

Often, people bully others after someone has bullied them. They just "pass it on." In this way, bullying is like a **contagious*** disease.

Bullying can be anywhere. This behavior may be in schools, families, work places, and sports teams. There may

be bullying among government workers, **politicians***, police, or business people.

Who are the targets* of bullying?

A bully's targets are often people who are weaker, smaller, or different in any way. Bullies may choose to hurt a person who doesn't have a group of friends to **stand up for*** him or her. But a popular student with good grades can also be the target of cyberbullying.

Bystanders*

A person who sees another person acting like a bully, may know that this is wrong. They may stand by and watch. They do nothing. The bystander may be afraid that the person who is bullying others will later bully them.

Results of bullying

We all need to feel safe at school, at home, at work, or in our neighborhood. Targets of bullies lose their feeling of safety. They lose **self-confidence***. They can become sick. They may **avoid*** work, school, or sports where they have been bullied.

In recent years, some young people **committed suicide*** after others had bullied them for a long time. Other young people who were bullied became angry and dangerous. They even killed some people.

Can schools prevent* bullying?

Most states have laws against bullying and cyberbullying. Targets of bullying do not have to feel **ashamed***.

If you are bullied by others, you can say. "Stop that. That hurts." Or, "Please **treat me with respect***."

If bullying continues, then you should **report*** the bullying to a teacher. If the bullying does not stop, report it again. Parents can come into school to report repeated bullying to the **principal***.

State laws say that teachers and principals must take action against bullying that they see or that someone reports to them. Bullying

hurts many people. It hurts the person who bullies as well as the target of bullying.

Schools may **require*** **counseling*** for the student who bullies others. They may **suspend*** or **expel*** a student who bullies or who start fights. They may send students who bully to a different school.

What can you do?

If you see someone bullying another student, speak up. Say, "Stop that. That's bullying."

Schools can teach students to **respect*** others. Schools can teach students to stand up and say or do something to stop bullying when they see it. Students can stand next to the target, or try to **protect*** the target. They can report the bullying.

Parents and teachers can teach children to **accept*** others who are different. They can help young people feel **compassion*** for themselves and others.

Schools can **reward*** acts of kindness. They can let students start **projects*** for helping others. When we help others, we can enjoy others and feel their **appreciation***.

This appreciation can fill the need to feel special and important. It's a much better way than bullying.

Let's talk about it.

1. What is bullying?

2. What are some examples of bullying?

3. Why do you think some people behave like bullies?

4. What can a person do if he or she is being bullied?

5. What can you do if you see someone bullying another person?

6. What do you think a school should do about bullying?

Using new words:
Match the word with its meaning.

_____ 7. a feeling of being not as good as others

_____ 8. showing thanks for good things done

_____ 9. using the Internet to make fun of people

_____ 10. a comment to make a person feel bad

_____ 11. able to spread from one person to
another, like an illness

A. cyberbullying

B. inferiority

C. insult

D. contagious

E. appreciation

Write a word in each sentence to make it correct. Choose from this list:
principal   reward   compassion   damage   anonymous

12. A person may try to be _____ when he or she uses
a computer to bully another person.

13. The _____ is the manager of a school.

14. Students will work harder when they can see a _____.

15. We have to learn to feel _____ for other people
who are different from us.

16. Insults and bullying can _____ a person's feeling of
safety and self esteem.

7. High School Graduation*

State requirements*

Each *state* sets requirements for graduation from high school. A *town* can have more, (but not fewer), requirements.

In order to graduate high school, a student must take the courses that their state and **local*** school district require. They must also take some **electives***.

Students who move to the United States can get **credit*** for many of the high school courses they completed in their home countries. They must bring in a school **transcript*** with a translation to English for the new school to **evaluate***.

(Don't be confused: In South America, the word *colegio* means *high school*.) In English, *college* means the two or four years of education after high school. A *college* may be part of a **university***.

How long can a student go to high school?

The **average*** age at graduation is 18. Most states **allow*** students to get free **public*** education up to the age of 19 or 20. A few states allow students up to age 21 or 22.

Students older than the state **maximum***

State of California minimum* requirements:

- English: 3 years

- Mathematics: 2 years
  including algebra

- Science: 2 years

  1 year of biology and
  1 year of a **physical science***

- Social Studies: 3 years

  1 year of U.S. history and
  geography*

  1 year of world history,
  culture, and geography
  1/2 year of American
  government
  1/2 year of **economics***

- Physical Education: 2 years

- Arts, foreign language, or **career***
  technical education: 1 year

City of San Bernardino, California minimum requirements:

- English: 4 years
- Mathematics: 3 years
- Science: 3 years
- World Geography: 1 year
- World History: 1 year
- Economics: 1/2 year
- American Government: 1/2 year
- Art or Foreign Language: 1 year
- Physical Education: 2 years
- **Career Development***: 2 years
- Electives:
  4 years

---

age may not **attend*** free public high school. They must take classes with adults.

Graduation Day

Students do many things to prepare for graduation day. They have to pass tests. They **rehearse*** for the graduation ceremony. They practice marching, singing, and how to receive their **diplomas***. Students buy the class **yearbook***. They **autograph*** each others' books and write special notes. They ask teachers and classmates, "Will you sign my book?"

The graduates wear traditional caps called **mortarboards***. The mortarboards have tassels that hang from the right side. They wear long **gowns*** over their clothing. (Students **rent*** these just for the day of graduation.) The graduating class walks slowly into the **auditorium***. Traditional music, usually the *Pomp and Circumstance March* by Sir Edgar Elgar plays as they walk in.

At the ceremony, the **salutatorian*** of the class welcomes parents, friends, and teachers. The **valedictorian*** of the class speaks about the future. A guest speaker gives a speech to **inspire*** the graduates.

The graduates (or the school **chorus***) may sing the school song. They may sing the *Star Spangled Banner* or some other **patriotic*** song. The school band plays some favorite music.

Receiving the diplomas

Then, graduates receive their diplomas. An important person in local education gives out the diplomas. This is often the president of the **board of education***. That person calls the name of each graduate. The graduate walks on stage, shakes hands with the right hand, and receives the diploma with the left hand. He or she says, "Thank you," and walks off the stage.

When there are hundreds of graduates, the **audience* holds their applause*** until a whole row of students receive their diplomas. When all the graduates have received their diplomas, they move the tassel on their mortarboards to the left side.

(The tassels are on the left for college graduates, who move them to the right when they graduate.) After the ceremony, the graduates may toss their caps in the air.

There may be a photographer to take photos of the graduates with their diplomas. Parents and friends take a lot of photos. Students say good-bye to friends they may not see again.

The graduates receive gifts from parents and other **relatives***. They may have parties with family and friends.

It's important to keep a diploma in a safe place. Students make copies if they need to show them to **potential* employers***. Many graduates **frame*** their diplomas and hang them on a wall.

Most colleges require that **applicants*** have graduated high school. Many jobs require that as well.

Monroe-Woodbury Central High School
DIPLOMA
PRESENTED TO
Elizabeth Claire Eardley
June 21, 1956
DATE
SIGNATURE

Let's talk about it.

1. Are you in high school now? What courses are you taking? (Or, what courses did you take in high school?)

2. What are your school's requirements for graduation?

3. Did you get credit for courses you took in your home country?

4. Did you graduate from high school in your home country? Tell about it.

5. How old were you? What were the requirements for graduating there?

6. What is a valedictorian? What does the valedictorian do at graduation?

7. What role does the salutatorian have at graduation?

Using new words:
Match the word with its meaning.

_____ 8. the smallest or lowest amount

_____ 9. a large room with seats, like a theater, where people can watch performances, graduations, etc.

_____ 10. the graduate who has the highest grade-point average

_____ 11. the document that shows that a person has completed the required courses

_____ 12. a document that lists the courses a person has completed at a school

A. diploma

B. valedictorian

C. minimum

D. transcript

E. auditorium

Write a word in each sentence to make it correct. Choose from this list:
requirements   inspire   patriotic   economics

13. _____ is the study of money, banking, and finances.

14. A speaker at graduation will try to _____ the new graduates to do well in life.

15. A _____ song is a song that shows love for one's country.

16. States have _____ for high school graduation.

8. Higher Education

The last year of high school is a busy time for students. They must make plans to get a job or prepare for college or other higher education. A high-school **diploma*** is important. Colleges, the **Armed Services***, and many training programs **require*** a high school diploma.

About 7% of students in the U.S. leave school without graduating. The **drop out*** rate is higher for English language learners. They drop out because of the difficulty of learning subjects in a new language. Many of them need to start earning money to help their families.

Teachers **urge***: **Invest*** in yourself. Get all the education you can. There is a second chance to get a high school diploma. Students of any age can take a General Education Development (GED) test. Many colleges **accept*** the GED as equal to a high school diploma.

Advanced placement*

Some high schools give college-level classes. Students can get college credit if they pass these advanced courses.

Guidance counselors*

School guidance counselors help students make decisions about their future. The guidance counselors help students **apply*** for **scholarships*** and **financial aid***.

A student and his or her parents should make an appointment to speak with the school guidance counselor. They talk about the student's interests and **abilities***. They can help students choose the best way to continue their education or get a job.

Career Day

Most high schools have one or more career days. People in different **occupations*** come to talk about their jobs. Students can ask about the **pluses and minuses*** of each job. Ask "What training or education did you need for this job? What do you like about it? What are things you don't like about the job?"

Students should not **rely*** completely on a guidance counselor or Career Day. The government has a good **resource*** to help people decide on a **career***: *Occupational Outlook Handbook**. It tells **salaries*** and requirements for hundreds of occupations. It tells which jobs will disappear in the future and which occupations will need more workers.

College

About 66 percent of American high school students go on to college. College can prepare a student for a **profession*** in teaching, engineering, science, medicine, law, coaching, or business management. College can prepare students for law school, medical school, and other **professional*** schools. Professional degrees take four to eight years.

Students take special exams to get into college (**SAT*** or **ACT***). There are free practice aids at **https://www.khanacademy.org/sat**. Some college programs require SAT tests in certain subjects. Foreign-born students must take the TOEFL [TOH f'l] (Test of English as a Foreign Language). Colleges may require a high score to admit students. They may require the student to take **ESL*** classes.

Technical* schools

More than two thirds of the jobs in the United States do not require a college degree. Some of these jobs pay very well.

The U.S. has needs for workers with technical skills such as computer programming, **medical technology***, construction, **mechanics***, auto repair, cooking, heating and air conditioning, and **welding***. Technical school programs can take six months to four years.

Scams*

Some technical schools and trade schools are only in business to make a **profit***. They advertise on TV and on billboards. They have **high-pressure*** sales people who call themselves "counselors." They lie! They say their programs are **accredited***. The tuition costs are very

high. The counselors help a student apply for government grants and student loans. The education is poor and the teachers are not good. Students can't get jobs after the program. They are left with a lot of debt.

Investigate* a school before you apply. Ask your guidance counselor, and talk to **current*** students at the school and graduates of the school. **Google*** the name of a school, location, and the word *complaints*. This may help you see if there are problems.

On-the-job training

Some young people learn job skills while they are working. They may start "at the bottom" of a large organization, such as a telephone company, or a hotel or **restaurant chain***. They work at low-paying jobs. The company may train

them. Later, the company may **promote*** hard-working employees to management positions with better pay.

Workers may **switch*** to a new job when they find a better one. It is **customary*** to give **two-weeks notice*** before leaving.

Some **unions*** have **apprenticeship*** programs. In such programs, a person can work with an **expert***. That is how many people have learned carpentry, **plumbing**,* electrical work, bricklaying, **masonry***, or **cabinet making***.

Students can learn skills in adult education courses and self-study programs. They can take courses on the Internet, too.

Let's talk about it.

1. Why is the last year of high school a busy time for students?

2. Why is a high school diploma important?

3. How can a person get a high school diploma if they drop out of high school?

4. Have you had a Career Day at your school? Tell about it. Or, tell the class about your career.

5. What kinds of careers do colleges and universities prepare a person for?

6. What kinds of careers do technical schools prepare a person for?

7. What kind of career would you like for yourself?

8. What is on-the-job training?

9. What have you learned at any jobs you have had?

Using new words:

Match the word with its meaning.

_____ 10. a job or career

_____ 11. the amount of money a person earns

_____ 12. a way to learn on the job

_____ 13. a person at school who advises students about college

_____ 14. a plan to fool people into giving money for something with no value

_____ 15. a test to get into college

A. guidance counselor

B. occupation

C. apprenticeship

D. SAT

E. scam

F. salary

Write a word in each sentence to make it correct. Choose from this list:
apply   investigate   promoted   scams   require

16. If you _____ to a college, you need to have a high school diploma.

17. Before you go to a technical school, _____ it online. Ask students at that school what they think of it.

18. Some colleges _____ students to take the SAT or the ACT tests.

19. A person can be _____ to a management position after a few years experience.

20. Some technical schools do not give a good education. They are _____ to get students' and the government's money.

9. Paying for College

There are many reasons to go to college. A **liberal arts*** education includes language, **literature***, history, **philosophy***, physical education, and some science and math. These courses **improve*** a person's **ability*** to think. They make a person **well-rounded***. They help to enjoy the world, and to make lifelong friends. A liberal arts education helps a person to make better decisions, **contribute*** to society, and be a better citizen.

If you hope college will also help you to **earn a living***, you must choose courses that will also lead to a **career***.

College is expensive. It is an **investment*** in your future. College costs include **tuition***, room and **board***, books, fees, a computer, transportation, insurance, and laundry. A single textbook can cost $150 or more. A student might need five or more textbooks every **semester***.

The cost in 2016 for tuition at a state college **ran*** from $5,000 to $15,000 per year for **residents*** of the state. Out-of-state and international students pay more. The cost at a private college ran from $20,000 to $45,000 per year.

There is another cost of college: This is the **income*** a student *doesn't* earn while he or she is **attending*** college. That might be $20,000 or more a year.

Which degrees lead to good jobs?

A **bachelor's degree*** in English, art, music, **anthropology***, **sociology***, psychology, women's studies, or history are "step one" to further education. Alone, such degrees don't lead to good jobs. A person may need three or four more years of education in those fields to get a job such as teaching at a university.

College **majors*** that lead to good paying jobs are **STEM*** courses: (Science, Technology, Engineering, and Math). There are jobs in the fields of chemistry, biology, accounting, geology, web design, computer software development, business, and economics. Students who want to go on to medical school must also take many science classes.

Paying for higher education

Even students from **high-income*** families need help to pay college costs. Students can **apply*** for **financial aid*** at the same time that they apply to each college.

A student may apply for a *scholarship** for **excellence*** in some field—such as good grades, **athletic*** ability, service to the school, musical talent, or other ability.

Students with financial need may get a **grant*** to pay part of college expenses. The amount of the grant is **based on*** the student's family income. The U.S. government gives **Pell Grants*** to students from low-and middle-income families. Colleges also give grants to some students. Students do not have to pay back grants and scholarships.

Students and their family fill out the **FAFSA***. The FAFSA is an application **form*** that asks about the students' family income. A copy of the FAFSA goes to each college that the student applies to.

After a college **accepts*** a student, it will tell of the financial aid the student may get, This could be a **combination*** of scholarship, loan, grant, and a work-study program. A work-study program gives a student a part-time job to help pay costs. The college **reserves*** jobs in the cafeteria, library, offices, and other places for their work–study students.

Students may get student **loans*** from the government or from a private bank. Students have to pay these loans back after they leave school. Many college students graduate with a large **debt*** to pay back.

What happens if students **drop out*** of college? They are in a difficult situation. They have a large debt, but they don't have a good job to help pay for it.

Many students graduate college with debts of $30,000 to $200,000. It can take **decades*** to pay it back!

Choosing a career

Do you want a good future? Then plan carefully. Get the most education and best **skills*** you can while you are young and single. It takes much longer to get an education when you must **support*** a family.

The government **Occupational Outlook Handbook*** describes thousands of jobs. It tells about each job and the education or skill you need to get that job. You can learn the yearly pay for the jobs. You can learn the future need for those jobs.

There is a need for **blue-collar*** workers, too. Carpenters, plumbers, electricians, and welders can earn a good living without a college degree.

Sadly, many college graduates have to take jobs as waiters, bartenders, or baby sitters. They work in call centers, McDonald's, and other low-paying jobs. Their knowledge of English literature, the history of the world, women's studies, or sociology doesn't translate to good jobs.

Graduates who can speak, read, and write two languages **have an edge***. Spanish, East Asian languages, and Arabic are good choices for the near future. On the other hand, there is not a strong need for people **bilingual*** in French, Italian, Latin, or ancient Greek. There is no **demand*** for these languages in the business world.

College on a tight budget*

The cost of tuition at **community colleges*** is much lower. You can live at home and **commute*** to classes. You can do the first two years at a community college. Then you can **transfer*** to a four year college.

It will help to have good grades (A's) in your subjects if you want to transfer to a good college. You may get a scholarship to help pay the costs. A good, expensive college might give you more financial help than a less expensive college.

Let's talk about it.

1. What is a liberal arts education?

2. What are the values of a liberal arts education?

3. Which of these college courses would you enjoy (Or did you enjoy)?
   (Circle them.)

   World history, English literature, calculus, astronomy, chemistry, anthropology, psychology, women's studies, geology, biology, French, Spanish, Chinese, computer science, accounting, engineering, theater arts, music composition, political science, constitutional law, public speaking.

4. What community college is near you? _____ What does tuition cost there? _____What does tuition cost at a state college in your state? What does it cost at a private university?

5. What career seems interesting to you? What do you think would be enjoyable about it? What does it pay?

6. Where would you get education or training for that career?

Using new words:
Match the word with its meaning.

_____ 9. spending money and time to get something better in the future

_____ 10. one half of a full school year is a

_____ 11. the students who leave school without graduating

_____ 12. a person who lives in an area

_____ 13. a period of ten years

_____ 14. money that is borrowed

A. semester

B. drop out

C. investment

D. loan

E. decade

F. resident

Write a word in each sentence to make it correct. Choose from this list:
grants   majors   debt   income   support   excellence

15. A person with a family needs a good job to _____ them.

16. The U.S. government gives Pell _____ to students from low-income families.

17. A student who _____ in Spanish takes Spanish literature, Spanish grammar, Spanish poetry, and Spanish composition classes.

18. Many students graduate college with a large _____. They have to pay back loans.

19. The FAFSA form asks questions about a family's _____.

20. A person might get a scholarship for _____ in sports, music, art, or academics.

10. Friendship in the United States

How do people make friends?

Small children make friends easily. They play side by side and do things together. Children in elementary school make friends at school, in their neighborhood, and among family members. Children may change from one set of friends to another. Friendship is **based on*** enjoying the same games, living in the same neighborhood, or belonging to the same after-school clubs such as the **Cub Scouts***, **Brownies***, **4–H Club***, or sports activities. Parents may arrange "**play dates***" for their children whose friends do not live nearby.

In high school, **teens*** may belong to a group of friends and also have best friends. People choose friends who have the same ideas about studies, sports, music, **hobbies***, and activities. Girlfriends often share

personal **details*** of their lives. They talk, **chat***, or **text*** about their activities, **crushes***, homework, music, favorite stars, and their **opinions***. They **post*** their thoughts and opinions on Facebook. They post photos on **Pinterest*** and **Instagram***. Girls' friendships involve a lot of talking and listening. This can make it difficult for English language learners to make friends with American teen girls.

Boys and girls who are good in **athletics*** may find friends easily. They only need to talk about the game they are playing.

Most schools have after-school activities. Students can join **clubs*** and play in sports or games.

Students who are new in school may be **lonely***. They find it difficult to make friends. This is especially true for teens from another culture and teens who don't speak English well.

Newcomers often make friends with people who speak the same language. Students often find friends in their **ESL*** classes. All of these students are going through an **adjustment*** to the U.S. They have difficulty with English. This gives them something **in common***.

Friends or groups of friends **hang out*** together. They may go to parties, sports events, movies, and other social gatherings together. A person may invite a friend to visit their home for supper. There may be birthday parties. Friends may have **sleepovers*** at each others homes.

Peer pressure*

Teens in a group may dress alike. They want the same kind of shoes. They may color their hair or get **body piercings*** or **tattoos*** to be like their friends.

American young people have a lot of freedom. However, teens don't always make **wise*** choices for their health or future. Young people can get into trouble together more than they would alone. There are many dangers, such as under-age drinking, using marijuana or other drugs, early sex, unsafe sex, pregnancy, and gang activities. Teens may feel peer pressure to go against their parents' rules.

Parents want to meet their children's friends and the parents of the friends, if possible. They need to know what their children are doing. Parents need to keep their teens safe and **guide*** them to wise decisions.

Adult friendships

Years ago, it was a custom to welcome a person who moves into a neighborhood. Neighbors came to the door of a new neighbor to say hello. That custom is now **rare***. People have become too busy. There's also a fear of strangers.

Adult friendships take more time. People who see each other every day may smile and say "Good morning." However, they may be too busy to have new friends. They may have a job, a family, and all the friends they need. They may have no time for new friends.

People who live in the **suburbs*** may not see their neighbors often. Members of a religious group may make friends in their church, **synagogue***, temple, or **mosque***. Parents may make friends with other parents when they are at the playground with their children. Workers make friends at work.

Adults join groups such as **Toastmasters***, book discussion groups, political groups, neighborhood associations, and other **local*** organizations. They may volunteer at a library, school, hospital, or **animal shelter***. Most towns have adult education centers. People can take classes to learn cooking, car repair, woodworking, gardening, games, sports, languages, and many other subjects.

What do we call our friends?

A girl or woman may call other girls *girlfriends*. A girl will not call a boy a *boyfriend* unless they are **dating***.

Boys and men call their friends *friends*, *buddies*, or *pals*, but not *boyfriends,* unless they are both **gay***. If a boy has a friend who is a girl, whom he is not dating, he just calls her a *friend*  or *buddy*. A gay couple may refer to each other as *my partner*. (However, this might be confused with *business partner.*)

He's my boyfriend and *She's my girlfriend* mean *We are a* **couple***. We are **going steady***.

A man and woman (or boy and girl) who are friends but are not dating may say that they have a **platonic*** friendship. That is, not **romantic***. *Friends with **benefits*** means that a couple have sex sometimes, but they are just friends. They are not in love and have no plans for the future together.

Let's talk about it.

1. Do you make friends easily?

2. What are some friendships based on? What are the qualities of a good friend for you?

3. How are boys' friendships different from girls' friendships?

4. What might be some parents' rules about their children's friends?

5. What places are good for meeting people who have interests similar to yours?

6. Do you have a good friend? How did you meet?

7. How do peer groups pressure each other? Are these pressures always good?

8. What pressures do you feel from your group of friends?

Using new words:
Match the word with its meaning.

_____ 9. to spend time with someone

_____ 10. not very common

_____ 11. an area outside of a city

_____ 12. art on a person's body

_____ 13. a romantic feeling about someone who does not know about it

_____ 14. dating one person and that person only

A. going steady

B. crush

C. hang out

D. rare

E. suburb

F. tattoo

Write a word in each sentence to make it correct. Choose from this list:
   buddies   wise   volunteer   adjust   peer pressure

15. Teens may feel _____ to do things they would not usually do.

16. Teenagers don't always make _____ decisions.

17. One way to meet people is to _____ at a school, library, or animal shelter.

18. _____ are friends who have some of the same interests.

19. It takes a while to _____ to a new school or to life in the United States.

11. Gender* in the United States

Men's jobs, women's jobs

Many newcomers are surprised at the jobs men and women do in the United States. Some are **shocked*** the first time they see a man teaching **kindergarten*** or a woman driving a big city bus.

The past 50 years have brought equal **opportunity*** in many jobs in the United States. Laws say that **employers*** may not **discriminate*** by gender. Many top universities were once for men only. They are now open to women. Universities that were for women only now **accept*** men.

Women have entered **occupations*** that used to be for men only—letter carrier, police officer, fire fighter, **security guard***, construction worker. Women are also in **professions*** that used to be for men only: engineer, lawyer, TV news reporter, dentist, astronaut, and **surgeon***, for example.

Today, women are business managers and **professionals*** in every **industry***. Women have started their own businesses. Women have been elected mayors of cities, governors of states,

and members of Congress. In 2016, Hillary Clinton was the first woman **nominated*** by a **major*** political party to **run*** for president.

Men do not have to be the only **breadwinner*** in the family. They have more choices. They are free to choose jobs such as **secretary***, elementary teacher, or nurse. It's now OK for men to show their feelings. They can spend more time with their children. In some families, the wife

goes out to work. The husband can be the **homemaker*** or a stay-at-home dad. In many families, both partners share the responsibilities of earning a living, caring for the children, and doing **chores***.

Only men need to **register*** for **Selective Service***. Some people say that women should register, too, if they want to be **treated*** equally.

Employers must treat male and female workers the same. Large companies must give a woman six weeks time off when she has a baby. Those employers must also give a *man* time off to care for a new baby in the family.

Same-sex relationships

After the **women's liberation movement*** came the **gay*** liberation movement.

Fifty years ago, most gay men and women did not tell people about their attraction to the same sex. Police arrested people who were **openly*** gay. There were laws against serving alcohol to gay people. Doctors said that **homosexuality*** was a mental illness. Churches said same-sex behavior was a **sin***.

On June 28, 1969, police **raided*** a gay bar, the Stonewall Inn in Greenwich Village in New York City. For the first time, gay people fought back against the

police. A **riot*** started. The police called for help. The riots went on for six days.

That marked the beginning of a gay liberation movement. Gay people "**came out of the closet***." They organized groups to end **discrimination*** against gay and **lesbian*** people. Many famous gay men and lesbian women stopped hiding their **sexual orientation***. Gay **Pride*** parades on June 1 celebrate the "Stonewall Uprising."

According to Statistica.com, in 2013, 1.5% of adult women in the U.S. said they were lesbian; 1.8% of males said they were gay. This number is probably higher. Many gay people do not answer such questions.

Many states had laws *against* same-sex marriage. In 2016, the United States Supreme Court said that those laws were **unconstitutional***. Gay people in the United States may have the full **legal*** protection of marriage if they choose to marry.

There are still strong feelings about this. The Catholic Church and other religions say that marriage is between one woman and one man. They say that same-sex marriage is a "sin against God's law."

Transgender*

A few people grow up feeling that they are living in the wrong body. They feel that their minds are male, but their bodies are female. Or *vice versa**.

They **prefer*** to dress and behave as their feelings tell them is correct. Some of them want to appear as the gender they **identify with***. These transgender people often have **hormone*** treatments and **surgery*** to change their gender **characteristics*** such as voice, muscles, beard, body hair, and breasts.

Transgender people want to be on sports teams as the gender they identify with. They want to use the bathroom, **locker room***, and other **facilities*** for the gender they identify with. They also want people to use the pronoun *he* or *she* that they prefer.

Caitlin Jenner was once *Bruce* Jenner. As Bruce, he was a gold medal winner in the 1976 Olympics. Jenner married three times. He is the father of six children.

Since 2015, Jenner is experiencing life as a woman, Caitlin. She has helped people to understand and learn to accept transgender people.

Let's talk about it.

1. In your home country, what are jobs for men only?

2. What jobs are for women only?

3. In the U.S., what are jobs that women cannot do? What jobs can men not do?

4. What kind of work would you like to do when you finish school? Can a person of either gender do this job?

5. Would you be able to do this work in your home country? Why or why not?

6. Has your home country ever had a woman leader? Tell about her.

7. Do gay people in your home country have the right to marry the person they love?

8. What problems do you think transgender people have in life at school?

Using new words:

Match the word with its meaning.

_____ 11. treat a group differently from another group

_____ 12. a career such as teacher, doctor, engineer

_____ 13. announce that one is gay

_____ 14. a feeling of being glad for what one is or what one has accomplished

_____ 15. vice versa

A. discriminate

B. the other way around; the opposite way

C. profession

D. come out of the closet

E. pride

Write a word in each sentence to make it correct. Choose from this list:
chores   occupations   breadwinner   gender

16. Women have entered _____ that used to be for men only.

17. Childcare, shopping, cooking, washing dishes, and cleaning are examples of home _____.

18. The person who earns money to support the family is a _____.

19. Today in the U.S., it is illegal to discriminate on the basis of a person's _____.

12.

Love and Romance

Sooner or later, a person wants to choose a life partner—or at least a **long-term*** sweetheart. Americans choose partners **based on*** **attraction*** and **common*** interests.

A **couple*** spend time together in different activities to learn if they will be **suitable*** partners for each other. They **date***. They might go for walks, go swimming, play cards, video games, tennis, or other sports, go out for dinner, go dancing, go to the movies, talk, or study for exams together.

Most dating is between young people before they get married. But some marriages end in divorce. Older people might re-enter the **dating scene***.

Dating manners and customs in the U.S. **vary*** a great deal. There are differences for each age, **ethnic*** group, economic class, religion, and education. The ways to meet **potential*** partners changes, too, with new **technology***.

Many American teens want to begin dating. Most families have rules about dating, especially for their daughters. These are some common rules:

- No dating until you're 15 (or 16, or 18).
- You can go out with a group of friends, but not alone with a boyfriend or girlfriend.
- We want to meet the person you are dating before you go on a date.
- We want to know where you are going.
- No drinking. No smoking marijuana. No drugs.
- You have to be home by (10) p.m.

Some parents drive the dating couple to the movies or party or social event they are going to. Parents may **ground*** a teen for staying out past **curfew***. They may take away **privileges*** such as cell phones, TV or computer time, or use of the family car.

Some families want their children to date only people from the same race or religion.

Sexual activity

Sixty years ago, **virginity*** was valued for American women. **Chaperones*** watched over young couples. Many women waited for marriage before having sex. People married at a young age.

Today, values have changed. Many teenagers are sexually active as early as 14. Schools may have classes in sex education and family life. Students in those classes learn about sexual **intercourse*** and how babies are **conceived***. They learn how to **avoid*** pregnancy and how to avoid **sexually transmitted*** diseases (STDs). In some states, schools teach that **abstinence*** is the only way to **prevent*** pregnancy. Other states allow schools to teach about **contraception***. Family life classes have helped to lower the rate of teen pregnancy.

Same-sex romance

Today, young people **accept*** the fact that some people are gay. It's normal for some people to be attracted to someone of the same sex. **Gay*** and **lesbian*** couples date and fall in love, just like anyone else. Gay people are a small percentage of the population. That makes it harder to find a life partner. Many gay people move to large cities.

Where do people meet each other?

For young people, the easiest is in school, college, church, clubs, and the neighborhood. Sometimes friends **introduce*** two people or arrange a **blind date***.

People might meet someone at work. Work romances are not always a good idea. When a romance ends, someone might be hurt. That can have bad feelings in the workplace.

Meeting online

Many people use Internet **dating sites*** to meet others. Some good relationships have started this way. However, Internet meetings have dangers. One person may be looking for a long-term relationship. The other person may only want a **one-night-stand***.

A person has to be sure that the other person is honest, and even **sane***! A person might post the photo of an actor or model. Someone might use Internet dating to find a **victim*** for a **crime***.

Internet Dating Scams

Most people keep their personal information secret from someone they meet on the Internet. They do not tell their full name, their actual email address, and their telephone number.

There are online services that can check out a person's **background*** for a **fee***. It's possible to learn if the person is married, is deep in debt, or has a **criminal record***.

If a person decides to meet someone, they can **arrange*** a short afternoon meeting. It can be in a public place such as a coffee shop. They can tell a friend where they are going. They don't drink alcohol. They plan how to leave if they decide to end the date early.

Who pays for a meal or movie on a date?

People can agree ahead of time to "go Dutch." That is, each person pays for his or her own meal, drinks, movie ticket, etc. Or, the person who has invited might **treat*** the other. The other person can accept or **decline***. At a later date, the other person might pay.

How do you say "No thank you?"

It's good manners to say something like, "Thank you for asking. But I'm sorry, no."

How do you end a relationship?

Relationships are not easy. Love often brings **anxiety*** for one or both partners. No one wants to get hurt or to hurt someone else. But to find love, people take that **risk***.

Sometimes one person wants a relationship to continue, and the other person wants to end it. It's best to be honest, gentle, and firm. It's important to not lie about feelings. The other person has the right to look for a more suitable partner. "I'm sorry. This relationship isn't what I was looking for. You're an interesting person and I hope you find the right one for you." If the relationship was long term, you can add: "Let's stay friends, but not romantic friends."

Let's talk about it.

1. Do you have a sweetheart or life partner? Where did you meet?

2. What is dating? What activities are good for people who are just meeting each other?

3. How do couples meet each other in your home country?

4. What are some rules parents might have for their teenage children who want to date?

5. Does your school have classes in sex education? What is the purpose of such classes?

6. Who do you think should pay for the costs on a date, such as dinner or tickets to a movie? Why?

7. Why is it important to end a relationship carefully and gently?

Using new words:
Match the word with its meaning.

_____ 8. two people together; husband and wife

_____ 9. complete avoidance of some temptation

_____ 10. to pay for another person's dinner or expenses on a date

_____ 11. a person who is hurt in an accident or crime

A. couple

B. victim

C. abstinence

D. treat

Write a word in each sentence to make it correct. Choose from this list:
blind date   ground   curfew   risk   chaperone

12. "If you stay out after midnight, we're going to _____ you for a month," said Jonah's mother.

13. When Monica lived in Argentina, her parents did not let her go out without a _____.

14. My parents have set a _____ for me. I have to be home by 10 p.m.

15. It's not easy to take a _____. You might get hurt, lose money, or be in danger.

16. Jason met Louise on a _____. His friends fixed him up.

13. Getting Engaged*

In the United States, men and women do not need their parents' **consent*** to get married if they are 18 years old or older. A few men might follow an old **custom***: They ask a woman's father for **permission*** to marry his daughter.

After a **couple*** has known each other for some time (it could be years, or only weeks) one of them **proposes*** marriage. They may make this a very special **occasion.***

After a couple agree to marry, they are engaged. The man may give a gift (most often a diamond ring) to his sweetheart. She wears this engagement ring on her left hand, on the "ring finger" (the second smallest finger).

She is now a **fiancee***. He is the **fiance***. (Both are **pronounced*** the same: FEE ahn SAY.)

They may decide to live together first. If they are very **traditional***, they will wait until they are married.

Some couples have an engagement party to **celebrate*** with friends and family. They may receive gifts at this time. People say, "Congratulations!" "Lucky couple!" They ask questions, such as, "When is the wedding?"

How long from engagement to marriage?

The engagement can last from a few days to many years. During this time, the couple get to know each other better. They talk about their plans for the future. They want to know what the other person **expects*** in a marriage: *Do they want children? Where will they live? What religion will they be married in? Who will go out to work? How much will they be able to pay for rent or for a house?*

What if?

If the woman decides not to marry, she should return the ring to the man. If the man breaks the engagement, the woman often keeps the ring.

Waiting period

The couple go to the town clerk to get a marriage license. Some states require a waiting period of one or two days; other states do not. The couple may go to a **justice of the peace*** to be married. They may hire an **official*** to get married in their own home or a parent's home or friends' home.

A traditional wedding

If the couple want a traditional wedding, they may take a year to prepare for it. A traditional wedding is a very big event in the life of a couple and their families. Couples may follow some traditions and also **create*** their own events.

The couple must set a date and **reserve*** a church or **temple***. They must decide who will conduct the marriage ceremony. They must reserve that official's time. They may have meetings with **ministers***, **rabbis***, or **priests*** for **pre-nuptial*** counseling.

The couple decides who to invite. They find a **catering hall*** to have the **reception***. They decide the dinner **menu*** and the costs. They plan the music, the flowers, and many other details. The **bride*** shops for a wedding dress.

The couple pick out the rings they will **exchange*** during the wedding ceremony. They choose a **DJ*** or a band to play at the reception. They choose or create invitations and send them to the **guests*** a few months before the wedding.

All of these activities help the couple learn about each other's needs and wants. They may **argue***. They practice making decisions together.

Other people in the wedding

The **groom*** chooses his **best man*** and the **ushers***. The groom may wear a suit or rent a **tuxedo***. He may ask for **formal*** clothes for the ushers and best man.

The bride chooses her **bridesmaids***. The chief bride's maid is the **maid of honor***. (If this is a married woman, she is the **matron*** of honor.) These are relatives or friends. The bride chooses the bridesmaids' dresses.

Gifts and the bridal shower*

A month or so before the wedding, the maid or matron of honor plans a shower. This is a party where friends and family "shower" the couple with gifts. Usually the date of the shower is a secret from the bride. If you are invited to a bridal shower, don't mention it to the bride!

Many couples **register*** at a department store or other store. They make a list of things at the store that friends can choose to buy as gifts (sheets, glasses, towels, dishes, pots, CDs, books, etc.). The friends and family can go to the store to see the list, or they can choose a gift at the store's online website. When a person buys something on the list, the store removes that item from the list. Then other guests won't buy the same things.

You can get a gift from any other place, or give a gift card or cash.

The bachelor* party

The best man plans a bachelor party for the groom. This is traditionally one or two days before the wedding—the man's "last days of freedom." This party may be full of sex jokes, alcohol, surprises, and a **stripper***. The groom's friends **tease*** him a great deal at this party.

Some brides are invited to a **bachelorette*** party. There are all sorts of jokes. The women may go to see male strippers.

Who pays for the wedding?

Traditionally, the parents of the bride save their money to pay for a daughter's wedding. Today, many couples pay for their own wedding. The parents of the groom may pay for the **rehearsal dinner***.

Let's talk about it.

1. What is the purpose of an engagement?

2. How do people in your home country choose a life partner?

3. What do you think are good qualities for a life partner?

4. How long might an engagement be?

5. What is a traditional engagement gift for a woman from the person who proposes to her?

6. If a couple plan a traditional wedding, what are some of the things they must think about?

7. Why would an engaged couple register at a department or other store?

8. What is a bridal shower?

Using new words:

Match the word with its meaning.

_____ 9. a person who can perform marriages

_____ 10. practice for a ceremony or performance

_____ 11. the man who is getting married

_____ 12. to ask a person to get married

A. groom

B. justice of the peace

C. propose

D. rehearsal

Write a word in each sentence to make it correct. Choose from this list:
menu   formal   traditional   celebrate   bachelor

13. A man who has never been married is a _____.

14. Look at the _____ and choose something to eat.

15. Many older people like to do things in a _____ way.

16. It's fun to _____ a birthday, wedding, or other happy time.

17. The groom and ushers may wear _____ clothes such as tuxedos at the wedding.

14. A Traditional* Wedding

A wedding can be very simple. The **bride*** and **groom*** get a marriage license from the **town clerk***. They go with two **witnesses*** before an **official***. (This may be a minister, mayor of a town, captain of a ship, or **justice of the peace***.) They say their **vows***, and sign the license. The official **files*** the license with the town clerk.

A traditional Christian American wedding takes place at the **altar*** of a church. Many spring and summer marriages take place outdoors. Some couples want a wedding in a special location such as a beach in Florida or on an island in the Caribbean.

(For information about Jewish, Muslim, Buddhist, or other traditional weddings, see Wikipedia.com.)

The rehearsal* and the rehearsal dinner

The day or evening before the wedding, the couple rehearses with the official who will **perform*** the marriage **ceremony***. They practice how they will walk, where they will stand, and their other actions. This way, they will avoid making mistakes on the day of the wedding.

After the rehearsal, there is a rehearsal dinner for the members of the **wedding party*** and the out-of-town **guests***. There are **toasts*** and stories about the bride and groom.

The wedding

Saturday is the most popular day for weddings. The wedding may be in the late morning, midafternoon, or evening. As the guests arrive, **ushers*** greet them. They ask, "Are you for the bride or for the groom?" The groom's family and friends sit on the right side of the center **aisle***. The bride's family and friends sit on the left side. The ushers **escort*** the guests to their seats.

The wedding begins when the ushers escort the mother of the bride and the mother of the groom to their places in the front row of the **assembly***. Then the groom, the best man, and the officiant come to the altar from a side door. The best man holds the wedding rings. At some weddings, a young boy carries the rings. The groom stands at the altar and waits for his bride.

Music begins. An usher escorts the **maid*** or **matron of honor*** down the aisle. Then the **bridesmaids*** each walk with an usher. Following them, a young girl may **spread*** flower petals* on the aisle where the bride will walk.

Here comes the bride

The bride appears at the entrance to the church. The bride's father or other man in the family escorts the bride down the aisle. He is "giving her away." (Both parents may walk with the bride, or she may walk by herself.) Then Wagner's *Wedding March* from the opera *Lohengrin* begins. People may think these words to the music: *Here comes the bride, all dressed in white.* All the guests stand up to **honor*** the bride.

The bride then stands at the altar next to the groom.

The ceremony

The official gives a short talk about marriage. Friends may read special poems or short **chapters*** from **sacred*** books. The **choir*** or a **soloist*** sings the songs that the couple have chosen.

Then the couple say their wedding vows. The official asks, "Will you take this woman to be your wife? To love, honor and **cherish***, for richer or for poorer, in sickness or in health, until death do you part?"

The groom answers, "I will."

Then the official asks the bride the same question. The bride answers, "I will." The groom puts a ring on the bride's finger. The bride puts a ring on the groom's ring finger.

The official says, "I now **pronounce*** you husband and wife. You may kiss the bride."

The reception*

After the ceremony, the bride and groom leave the church. Guests outside throw **birdseed***, or **confetti***. They may blow bubbles.

The members of the wedding party form a line. Friends go down the line and **congratulate*** the bride and groom, their parents, and the ushers and bridesmaids. They say things such as: "Congratulations!" "You look lovely!" "It was a beautiful ceremony!" "Good luck!" "Thank you for inviting me!" Guests then go to the place for the reception. Meanwhile the bridal party **poses*** for photos.

At the reception, there is a **buffet*** or a full sit-down meal (or both). A **master of ceremonies*** (MC) announces each event at the reception. The best man **offers a toast*** to the bride and groom. Each person has a small glass of **champagne*** and drinks to the bride and groom.

The dancing begins. The bride and groom have their first dance together as man and wife. Then the bride dances with her father. The groom dances with his mother.

Then everyone may dance. There may be special group dances and ethnic dances.

The honeymoon*

The bride and groom often leave that night or the next day for a honeymoon. A honeymoon might be a weekend or one, two, or three weeks. Often it is to travel to some beautiful place, national park, or city that the couple have not been to before.

Let's talk about it.

1. What are some wedding traditions in your home country? Are there special clothes? Special foods? Special gifts?

2. What time of year is popular for weddings in your home country? Why?

3. Did you have a party when you got married? Tell about it. Or, tell about the wedding you would like to have.

4. Have you been to an American wedding? Tell about it.

5. Have you been to a wedding of some other nationality? Tell about it.

6. Where would you like to go on a honeymoon?

Using new words:
Match the word with its meaning.

_____ 7. a person who shows you to your seat

_____ 8. a person who is present to see an event

_____ 9. a meal that is "serve yourself"

_____ 10. the party after the wedding ceremony

_____ 11. to take good care of someone you love

_____ 12. a special vacation for the newly married couple

A. usher

B. cherish

C. buffet

D. reception

E. honeymoon

F. witness

Write a word in each sentence to make it correct. Choose from this list:
bridesmaids   vows   master of ceremonies   congratulate

13. The bride and groom say their marriage _____ at the altar.

14. Friends and family _____ the bride and groom after the wedding ceremony.

15. Women who help the bride before and during the wedding are

_____.

16. The person who announces events at a party is the

_____.

Dear Elizabeth,

I received an invitation to go to my neighbor's daughter's wedding. I have never been to an American wedding. What must I wear? Can I bring my boyfriend? What kind of gift is OK? What is **R.S.V.P.***?

John and Heather Romero
request the honor of your
presence at the marriage
of their daughter

Elizabeth Ann
to
Martin Carlson

at the First Christ Church
1400 Cycle Street,
Banford, Massachusetts

Reception to Follow.

RSVP

Chara

Dear Chara,

It is an **honor*** to be invited to a wedding. It's also an chance to have an interesting experience. You will learn a lot.

The invitation

R.S.V.P. are **initials*** for French words: *Respondez, s'il vous plait.* That means, "Please reply." It's important to answer quickly. The couple must know how many people will come for dinner at the **reception hall***. They may pay $50 to $150, or more, for each guest.

There is usually a little card and a stamped envelope that comes with the invitation. You can mail it back to your neighbor. Write "Yes, I will be happy to come. Thank you," and sign your name on the card. If you cannot **attend*** the wedding, write, "Thank you for inviting me. I'm sorry, I cannot come."

Did the envelope say "Chara *and guest*?" If it did, then you can invite your boyfriend.

If it did not say *Chara and guest*, then I'm sorry, your boyfriend is not invited to the wedding. Don't worry. You will meet new people. Have fun.

Ceremony* only

Some people invite neighbors and friends only to the church ceremony. Anyone might go to see the wedding at the church. The **reception*** is the private party for family and close friends of the bride and groom or their families. Not everyone is invited to the reception. It's often at a different **location***. *Reception to follow* means that you are invited to the reception.

Wedding gifts

If you go to the reception, you should get a gift for the couple. If you don't go to the wedding, a gift is **up to you***. The bride may have chosen a store that has many different kinds of gifts. You can ask "Is the bride **registered*** anyplace?" If she is, then you can go to the customer service counter in that store. Ask customer service for a list of gifts that the couple has made. You may be able to do this on the Internet at the store's website. You can choose a gift that is in your **budget***. (**Superstition***: Do not give knives as a gift.)

Many people give a money gift. The couple can buy what they need. Fifty to two hundred dollars is **common*** from two people. A check is OK, a gift card, or new bills. Put this in a wedding card. Be sure to sign your first and last name. Have your address

$100
Gift Card

inside the card as well, so the couple can send a thank you card.

At the church

Guests should arrive about 15 minutes before the time of the wedding. When you enter the church, an **usher*** greets you. In a Christian wedding, the bride's family and guests sit  on the left side of the church. The groom's family and guests sit on the right side. The usher will ask if you are there *for the bride* or *for the groom*. Then the usher will take your arm and **guide*** you to a seat.

The reception

At the reception, you may see a table with *hors d'oeurves* [or DERVES] (**appetizers***), drinks at the bar, and after that, a full-course meal. You don't have to wonder where to sit. There will be a table with name cards. Find  the card with your name. It will tell you the table where you may sit.

If you have brought a gift, you may put it at a table for gifts. If you have brought a card with cash or a check in it, look for a decorated box with an opening for envelopes. Or you can hold it until the bride comes to your table to thank the guests for coming. At that time, you can give the gift envelope to the bride.

When you sit at your table, say Hello to the other guests. Tell your name and ask their names. Guests make pleasant conversation, and tell stories and jokes.

Don't wait for people to talk to you. Speak up; ask questions. For example: *How do you know the bride? What did you think about the ceremony? Where will they live?* Compliment others. For example: *What a lovely dress. Your earrings are so interesting. I like your tie.*

Interesting things happen at a wedding.

The bride and groom cut the cake together. They feed cake to each other. They might make a **mess*** of it, just for fun.

The bride will **toss*** her **bouquet*** over her head to a group of unmarried women. They all try to catch it. You can join them. The person who catches the bouquet "will be the next to get married."

The bride sits on a chair in the middle of the room. The groom removes the **garter*** from her leg. He tosses the garter over his head to the **single*** men. The man who catches the garter must put it on the woman who caught the bouquet. This event is very funny.

The couple's friends **decorate*** the groom's car. They put on a sign, "Just Married." They tie empty cans to the back of the car. These make a lot of noise when the couple drive away.

Let's talk about it.

1. Have you been to a wedding in your home country? Tell about it.

2. Have you been to a wedding in the United States? Tell about it.

3. What kinds of things can you talk about with people you have just met at a wedding?

4. What advice would you give a couple who are getting married?

5. Are you married? If so, tell about your wedding. If you are not married, which would you choose: A traditional wedding and big party? Or just two witnesses and a justice of the peace?

6. Where do you think is a good place for a honeymoon? Tell about it.

Using new words:
Match the word with its meaning.

_____ 7. the flowers that a bride carries

_____ 8. a person who shows a guest to a seat in the church

_____ 9. a party after the wedding ceremony

_____ 10. a pretty elastic band that holds up a stocking

_____ 11. Please respond.

A. R.S.V. P.

B. reception

C. usher

D. bouquet

E. garter

Write a word in each sentence to make it correct. Choose from this list:
decorate   attend   appetizers   register   initials

12. Many people _____ the church to see the wedding ceremony.

13. Some bridal couples may _____ at a department store to help guests know what they need for gifts.

14. R.S.V.P. are _____ for *Respondez s'il vous plait.*

15. The groom's friends may _____ the car with streamers and empty beer cans after a wedding.

16. Food that a person eats before the main meal are _____.

16. Having a Baby in the United States

About four million babies are born in the United States each year. The **average*** age of first-time mothers is about 25.

Most American children are born into two-parent families. However, a large percent of babies (41%) are born to single women. Some of these single moms are teenagers. But most of them are women over 30 years old.

Prenatal* care

When a woman **suspects*** that she is **pregnant***, she may buy a pregnancy test kit at a drug store. If the test is **positive***, she'll make an appointment to see an **obstetrician/ gynecologist***. (For short, called an O.B/ G.Y.N.) After a blood test, the doctor can **confirm*** the pregnancy. The blood test will also tell the woman's **blood type*** and any problems that might affect the baby.

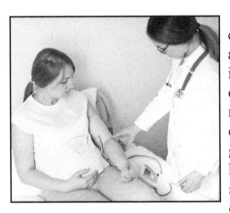

The doctor talks about the importance of good **nutrition***, exercise, and good health habits. (Stop smoking; don't use drugs; don't drink alcohol.) The doctor **recommends*** reading about pregnancy and childbirth. It's important to have monthly **prenatal*** check ups to see how the baby is growing. Prenatal visits to the doctor can catch any problems before they can do **harm***.

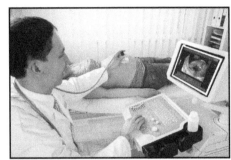

When the woman is eight weeks pregnant, the doctor can hear the baby's heartbeat. When she is four months pregnant, her doctor may do an **ultrasound***. This **procedure*** allows the doctor and mother to "see" the baby. With an ultrasound, the doctor can tell if there is more than one baby. Usually the doctor can see if the baby is a boy or a girl. Some parents don't want to know. They ask the doctor not to tell them.

As the weeks pass, and the baby grows, the woman gets a "**baby bump***." Department stores and special shops sell **maternity clothes*** for **expectant mothers***.

Prenatal classes

The mother- and father-to-be can take a child care class at a **local*** hospital or community center. They learn about caring for a baby. The woman learns special exercises to help her body get ready for **labor***. She can choose from different kinds of **pain relief*** or she can choose **natural childbirth***.

Some women want a **midwife*** to help them during **delivery***. Others choose an obstetrician. The mother decides if she will **breastfeed*** the baby.

A birth coach*

Some women have a birth coach to

help them during labor. This can be their husband, sister, mother, or a friend. The coach is trained to help the woman stay calm. He or she will coach the breathing technique that helps to **reduce*** pain.

Getting ready

At home, the parents set up an area for the baby. It may be in their room or in a special room for the baby. They clean the house.

A family member may plan a surprise **baby shower*** for the expectant mother. Friends and family bring gifts to get the new baby started in life: baby clothes, a **crib***, a **stroller***, blankets, **diapers***, bottles, **mobiles***, and many other things. Most of all, babies will need love and attention.

At the end of the eighth month, the woman gets ready to go to the hospital. She packs a small suitcase with clothes for herself and clothes for the baby.

Birth day

When the baby is ready to be born (generally after 270 days) the woman starts having **contractions***. They grow stronger and faster. She calls her doctor. The doctor tells the woman when to go to the hospital. Her **water may break***.

At the hospital, a nurse takes the woman to the labor room. She checks the mother's and the baby's heartbeats. She measures and **times*** the contractions. She takes the mother's **pulse***.

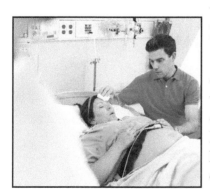

The husband or coach stays with the woman during labor. He tries to help her feel comfortable. If the woman has chosen some pain relief, an **anesthesiologist*** will give that to her.

The baby is born

The husband or coach holds the woman's hand. Her contractions push the baby out into the world. If the birth is very long and difficult, the doctor may recommend a **Caesarian delivery***. This is an operation to remove the baby, also called a *C-section.*

The doctor holds the baby while the husband (if he is present and if he wants to) cuts the **umbilical cord***.

The nurse gives the baby to the mother. After a few minutes, the nurse checks the baby for any problems. She measures and weighs the baby.

Choosing a name

Most parents choose a name for their baby in advance. They have a name for a boy and one for a girl (unless they know which it will be). Other parents wait until after a baby is born.

Later, the parents fill out a **birth certificate***. They write the baby's full name and the parents' names. The doctor writes the time of the birth and signs his or her name. The mother and child may leave the hospital after one or two days. If the mother had a C-section, she'll need more time in the hospital.

Let's talk about it.

1. Why does a pregnant woman need to have a blood test?

2. What are some things a woman should do when she is pregnant?

3. What are some things a pregnant woman should not do?

4. What can a pregnant couple learn from an ultrasound scan?

5. In your home country, how do parents prepare for childbirth?

6. What can a couple learn in prenatal classes?

7. What things will a baby need when it comes home?

8. What is the purpose of a birth coach?

9. How do parents in your country choose a name for a new baby?

Using new words:

Match the word with its meaning.

_____ 10. to be sure something is true

_____ 11. to give a person suggestions or advice

_____ 12. to think that something might be true

_____ 13. the timing of a heartbeat

_____ 14. to make smaller or less

A. suspect

B. confirm

C. reduce

D. recommend

E. pulse

Write a word in each sentence to make it correct. Choose from this list:
umbilical cord   procedure   Caesarian   midwife   maternity

15. A mother might choose to have a _____ instead of an obstetrician when her baby is born.

16. While a baby is inside the mother, it gets food and oxygen through the _____.

17. A pregnant woman might wear _____ clothes.

18. A doctor might do a _____ such as an ultrasound to check the growth of the baby before it is born.

19. In some cases, a doctor might perform a _____ delivery of the baby if the mother can't have a normal birth.

17. Other Ways to Become Parents

Some **couples*** do not have children. There are many possible reasons. It is **rude*** to ask them why.

Some couples have difficulty **conceiving***. They may try **fertility*** clinics. Eggs from the mother may be **fertilized*** **in vitro*** by her husband's **sperm***. A doctor transfers the **zygote*** to the mother's **uterus***.

A couple may find a **surrogate*** mother. The surrogate mother is pregnant with the couple's child until it is born. The couple pays her medical expenses and a **fee*** for her services.

There can be **legal*** and **moral*** questions around surrogate mothers: *What if the surrogate mother wants to keep the child? What if the child is born with a **disability***? What if the adopting couple divorce before the child is born? What if there are **twins***?*

Adopting* a child

Some couples adopt one or more children. Adoption is **common***, but there are not

many babies who need to be adopted in the United States. Many single mothers keep their babies. **Abortion*** is legal.

There are not many **orphans***.

The laws about adoption are different in each state. An adopting person or couple must show that they can **support*** a child. They must show that they have a **suitable*** home. They must show that they are healthy. The adoption process can take a very long time.

A person or couple who want to adopt a child may go to an adoption **agency***. They may advertise in newspapers or on the Internet. They may **consult*** a lawyer. Many couples adopt a child who is of a

different **nationality*** or race. They may get a child from places where there are more adoptable children, such as Russia, India, Korea, China, and South America.

Every child **deserves*** to be part of a family. However, some children do not get adopted quickly. They may have expensive medical problems. They may have **physical handicaps***. They may have been born to a mother who was addicted to drugs. It is not easy for a family to care for these children. The state government pays **foster parents*** to care for them. The

government pays for any medical problems.

Gay couples, unmarried people, and older people can adopt children.

Psychologists* say that children should learn that they are adopted. The parents should tell them when they are very young. Then it will not come as a surprise when they are

older. The family may celebrate "Adoption Day" as well as a birthday. The child learns that he or she is very special. The child feels how much his parents love him.

Parents who adopt children from other cultures may form a group with other adoptive parents. They help their children learn the customs and language of their birth parents. They celebrate the children's holidays together.

The birth **records*** of adopted U.S. children are **sealed*** by the court. This is to protect the birth mother. She did not want her family to know she had a child. No one can open the records.

However, some adult **adoptees*** want to know their family history. They want to know their nationality. They want to know if there is a health problem that can be **inherited***. They want to know if they have brothers or sisters. They say this is their right. They may search for years to find their birth mothers.

Some birth mothers let the court records stay open. They think some day their child may want to find them. Many birth mothers **regret*** giving away their child. They wait and hope that their child will try to find them. There are online services to help people find their **biological*** parents. One is **adoptionhelp.org**.

Some adoptees are finally able to meet their birth mothers. Brothers and sisters who were separated by adoption might find each other, too.

In a plan called Open Adoption, a mother can meet privately with adoptive parents. They may have a **contract*** between them to say what kind of relationship they will have. They may send a photo of the child each year, or allow visits on holidays. The adoptive parents may grant visiting rights for the biological mother.

Let's talk about it.

1. Is adoption common in your home country?

2. Why do you think people want to have children?

3. Some children are not adopted quickly. What might be some reasons?

4. Why should adoptive parents tell a child he or she is adopted? Why should they do that when the child is very young?

5. How can an adult adoptee find out who his birth parents are?

6. Why do some Americans adopt children from other countries? What do you think of this?

Using new words:
Match the word with its meaning.

_____ 7. children whose parents have died

_____ 8. passed from parent to child

_____ 9. feel sorry for what was done

_____ 10. a place for children when they have no family to care for them

_____ 11. two people; husband and wife

A. inherited

B. regret

C. couple

D. orphans

E. foster home

Write a word in each sentence to make it correct. Choose from this list:
disabilities   right   agency   adoptee   adoption

12. A couple may go to an adoption _____ to get help with adopting a child.

13. Children with physical _____ often are not adopted quickly.

14. Some families celebrate _____ Day as well as a child's birthday.

15. An adopted person is an _____.

16. Many adopted persons say it is their _____ to know about their birth parents.

18. Taking Care of Children in the United States

Children are important in the United States. It has been said that we are a "child-centered nation."

Children need love, warmth, sleep, food, drink, change of diapers, bathing, and teaching. Someone must protect **toddlers*** from serious falls, from **choking***, from sunburn, and from a hundred and one other harms. Children need **social skills*** and must learn how to **relate*** with people. They need to feel **secure***. They need to learn by watching other people, by playing with toys, listening to stories, and many other ways. They need to learn **limits*** to their **behavior***. They need lots of hugs and love.

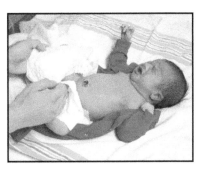

Who takes care of the children?

Years ago, stay-at-home moms, dads, grandparents, and older brothers and sisters took care of children's needs. These days, families are smaller, moms go to work, grandparents live far away, and dads may be absent. Still, family members are usually the best ones to take care of a small child.

It's important to choose the child's caregiver carefully.

There are babysitters or **nannies*** who

will come to your home. Some will live there if you have an extra room. There are sitters who watch children in their own home.

A babysitter must be **mature*** enough to know what to do in an **emergency***. He or she should know your wishes about how to care for your child. A home has many dangers for a small child. It's good to **childproof*** your home as well as the babysitter's home.

Day-care centers take care of many children and may be less expensive. In most states, day-care centers must be **licensed***. The state **inspects*** them for safety and cleanliness.

Early education

In low-income neighborhoods, the government may have a **Head Start*** program. This is a preschool. Licensed teachers there provide early education. Children can play with safe educational toys. They play games to learn social skills. They learn songs and hear stories that help build their **vocabulary***.

There are many toys for children.

Most toys will have a **label*** that tells what age they are good for. Small children often put things in their mouths. Toys with little parts are not **suitable*** for children under the age of three.

Part of a child's education is going for walks to a park or playground. A child must learn safety rules about the street.

Discipline*

It is natural that young children think everything in the world is theirs! They reach out to have each thing that looks interesting. It is a hard lesson to learn that the world does not belong to them. Children may **scream***. A parent can say, "You're so sad that you can't have that. It belongs to someone else. I can't give it to you. But you can have this..." (Bring along one or two of the child's own small toys to give at this moment.)

It used to be **common*** for parents to **spank*** a child. Now society **frowns upon*** spanking. A parent can be **arrested*** for hitting his or her own child! It's best to teach behavior through non-violent ways. "**Time out***" is a common practice to teach a child who **disobeys*** a parent's rules.

By age five, children are very **curious*** about everything. They ask questions and need answers. Parents can show the child that some answers can be found in books or by using a search engine such as **Google***.

Grandparents are a great help in raising children. They can give parents some rest.

They might **treat*** children in ways that are different from a parent's ways of doing things. Parents may want grandparents to use the same rules about children's behavior and foods to eat.

TV and computer games

Tired parents or babysitters let children watch TV. Many parents **limit*** TV time to one or two programs a day. There are good children's programs on PBS (Public Broadcasting System) with no **commercials***. Other networks show violence and many commercials.

Children as young as one year of age have **devices*** with computer games. Some of these games are **addictive***. They keep a child quiet. However, children who spend many hours with devices are not learning to relate to other people.

Feeding children

Children have very **sensitive* taste buds***. Many foods taste bad to them. It's important to let them taste new foods in small amounts. Children can slowly learn to like a **variety*** of food.

Children naturally like sweet things. It's important to limit sugar. Cookies, cake, desserts, candy, and such things **increase*** the desire for more. The United States has an **epidemic*** of overweight children. This can lead to early **diabetes***. Babies will enjoy **unsweetened*** applesauce and other fruit.

Let's talk about it.

1. Do you have children? What kinds of things must you do to take care of them? (Or, how do your parents take care of you?)

2. What are some dangers that parents or caregivers must protect a child from?

3. What are some things a small child must learn?

4. What are some ways to teach a small child that everything does not belong to him or her?

5. Is watching too much TV or playing computer games bad for a small child? Why or why not?

6. How might a parent help a child learn to eat many kinds of food?

7. How have your grandparents helped to take care of you?

8. Who cares for small children in your home country?

Using new words:

Match the word with its meaning.

_____ 9. a loud cry

_____ 10. words that a person has learned

_____ 11. interested in learning things

_____ 12. a child able to walk; a two year old

_____ 13. an advertisement on television or radio

_____ 14. a strong desire for candy and desserts

A. toddler

B. scream

C. curious

D. vocabulary

E. sweet tooth

F. commerical

Write a word in each sentence to make it correct. Choose from this list:
secure   epidemic   time out   suitable   childproof

15. Parents must make sure their home and any babysitter's home is
_____ so their child can't get hurt.

16. Babies need to feel _____ that someone will care for them.

17. There is an _____ of diabetes among overweight children.

18. Parents might use _____ as a way to teach children to
obey their rules.

19. Toys with small parts are not _____ for children under three
years old who might put them in their mouth.

19. Keeping Children Safe

Parents in the U.S. worry about their children. They try to **protect*** them from many kinds of dangers. There are laws to protect children, too.

One law is about riding in cars. Each state has different rules. For example, in New Jersey, an **infant*** up to age two and weighing less than 30 pounds must be in an infant seat that faces the **rear*** in the back seat.

Children under four years of age and weighing less than 40 pounds must be in a child seat. Children under eight years of age weighing less than 80 pounds must be in a **booster seat*** in the back of the car, if possible.

Safety **experts*** advise: Never buy a **second-hand*** child seat. It might have been in an accident. It may no longer be safe.

There are laws about children's toys. You can read **labels*** that tell what ages a toy is **suitable*** for. Toys with small pieces are **choking hazards***. Labels say, *Not for children under 3 years.* Items wrapped in plastic bags or sheets of plastic have labels that say, *Do not use as a child's toy.* (In the past, many babies died **suffocating*** with plastic on their face.) There are laws that parents may not leave children in a car on a hot day. The sun can heat up the inside of a car to 140 degrees Fahrenheit in a short time.

Some states have laws that say that children under twelve may not be left alone at home. A baby sitter for children must be at least 12 years old.

Parents or other adults may not physically **abuse*** children. There are laws against harsh **spanking*** or beating that leaves **bruises*** on a child. Physical abuse includes tying a child up, locking in a closet, and withholding food. There are laws against **neglect***, emotional abuse, and sexual abuse.

Child welfare agencies* may remove children from homes where the children are in danger.

Kidnappers* and child molesters*

One danger that parents worry about is **kidnapping***.

Parents want their children to know safety rules. But they don't want their children to be **overly*** fearful of the world. This is sometimes difficult.

Child molesters are people who act out on their sexual desires for children. They have ways to trick children into going with them. Teach your children to say *No* to any invitation to get into a car or enter a home. Explain that someone might lie to them. Some of the lies might be: "Your mother asked me to pick you up from school and take you home." "Your mother is hurt and can't come to get you. I'm going to take you to her." "Come and see baby kittens or puppies."

Teach children that they do not have to be polite to **strangers*** when you are not with them. They do not have to give people directions or answer any questions. Tell them that no one has the right to touch their bodies in private places (such as their breasts, **buttocks***, or **genitals***).

Tell your children that if they have any **doubts***, they should run away, and report it to you or to a teacher or police officer.

The National Center for Missing and **Exploited*** Children has advice for parents. "Always know where your young children are. Don't let small children go out alone. Know who their friends are. Know their friends' parents."

Be sure your young children know their address, town, and your telephone number. Speak with your children about their safety. Parents used to tell their children, "Never talk to strangers," or "Don't take candy from strangers." However, this is not enough. Children have to also know when a *neighbor*, a *family friend, parent, teacher, coach,* or *church official* is doing the wrong thing.

Teach your children to **refuse*** to go in a car or a house with another person without your **permission***, *even if it's someone they know.*

Some towns have "Escape Classes" to show children how to get away if anyone tries to take them. Find out more at **www. escapeschool.com**.

As children get older, they may meet people through the Internet. It's important to teach them never to give out their address or phone number or other personal information. Explain that there are people who pretend to be some friendly person. They may use photographs of someone else on a Facebook page and say it is them. They try to fool a child. Parents should carefully watch their children's use of **social media***.

AMBER Alerts*

One hundred to two hundred children are kidnapped by strangers and **murdered*** in the United States each year. This is a very small number for a population of 320,000,000. But it is a parent's worst **nightmare***. These cases make big **headlines*** in the news.

When a parent reports that a child is missing, the police start an "AMBER Alert." This is a national system to help find the child. This alert is posted on TV, radio, highway signs, **Twitter***, emails, and cell phones. Everyone in the country learns about the missing child. AMBER Alerts have helped save many children. (It is named for nine-year-old Amber Hagerman who was kidnapped while riding her bicycle in Arlington, Texas.)

Let's talk about it.

1. What is the law about babies and children when riding in a car?

2. What are laws about leaving children at home?

3. What are some laws about children's toys?

4. What are laws about hitting and disciplining a child?

5. What laws in your home country protect children?

6. What is an AMBER Alert?

7. What is some advice for parents to keep their children safe from kidnappers?

8. In what ways do child molesters fool children?

Using new words:
Match the word with its meaning.

_____ 10. to say *no* to an invitation

_____ 11. to get away from danger

_____ 12. a child under one year of age

_____ 13. a very bad dream

_____ 14. A very small toy can be a
_____ for a child under age three.

A. nightmare

B. infant

C. choking hazard

D. refuse

E. escape

Write a word in each sentence to make it correct. Choose from this list:
protect   pretend   kidnapped   abuse   booster seat

15. Parents need to _____ their children with good advice.

16. A child molester might _____ to be someone else on the Internet using social media to meet victims.

17. No one wants their child to be _____.

18. Parents may not _____ their children with harsh punishments.

19. A child between two and eight years of age should sit in a _____ in the back seat of a car.

Americans love animals. Many families have a pet of some kind. Forty percent of American families have a dog. Thirty percent have a cat. People may also keep birds, fish, **hamsters***, white mice, **gerbils***, snakes, and lizards.

In many homes, dogs and cats become "part of the family." They live inside the home. They eat in the same room as the family. The cat or dog may have its own bed to sleep in. It may sleep on a sofa or an armchair. It may even sleep in bed with a member of the family.

Newcomers, especially children, may want a pet, too. Families should know the costs, time, and problems of a pet.

A dog is a lot of work

Dogs need fresh food and water every day. They need to go for walks two or three times a day. Dogs need a lot of space to run and play.

It may take many weeks to **housebreak*** a puppy. A dog should not be left alone in a house for many hours. When the dog "**does his business***" (**defecates***; **poops***) outside, the owner must clean it up. Most owners carry a **pooper scooper*** when they walk their dog. They may take a plastic bag with them to collect the dog's poop. There is a **fine*** for owners who do not clean up after their dog.

A dog needs training to become "a good citizen." There are **obedience classes*** for dogs and their owners. The dogs' owners learn to teach the dogs to walk **calmly*** without pulling. The owners learn to teach the dogs to sit and stay, and to come when they are called.

Dogs need to learn not to jump on people and not to bite. There are videos on **YouTube** to show owners how to train their dogs.

Not everyone should have a dog

Many **landlords*** do not allow dogs in their apartments. Dogs can **damage*** doors and walls. They can **bark*** all day. Young dogs' teeth are growing. They need something to **chew*** on. Puppies may chew up shoes, boots, furniture, and electric wires. A **lonely*** dog or a dog that needs exercise may ruin things in the house.

Dogs need to be brushed and bathed regularly. Dog hair gets on people's clothes and the furniture. Someone in the family may have **allergies*** to dog hair.

Cats

A cat, on the other hand, can get along during the day without **disturbing*** the neighbors. It's easy to train a cat to use a **litter box***. A cat can be left home alone during the day while the family goes to work or school.

However, landlords don't like cats either. A cat's **urine*** has a very strong smell. It's hard to remove from carpets or furniture. Cats' **claws*** get itchy as they grow. Cats need a **scratching post***. A cat might **shred*** the sofa and other furniture with its claws.

You need to brush a cat with long hair everyday. Many people are **allergic*** to cat hair.

Laws about pets

Both dogs and cats need a **license*** from the town. They must have **vaccinations*** against several kinds of dog or cat diseases. They must get **rabies shots*** every one or two years.

Pets should see a **veterinarian*** (vet) for a checkup every year. Female dogs and cats should be **spayed*** so they can not have

babies. Male dogs and cats should be **neutered***. In many states, a dog that bites people may have to be **put down*** (**euthanized***).

Where do people get their pets?

There is an **overpopulation*** of dogs and

cats in the United States. Many of these animals are **abandoned*** by their owners. Children may cry to have a pet. They may lose interest in the pet after a few months. A family may move and not be able to take the dog with them. These unwanted pets wind up in an **animal shelter***. If no one **adopts*** them in a short time, they are euthanized.

People may adopt a pet from a shelter. There is an adoption **fee***, plus a fee to neuter the pet. It's important to know a dog's personality before adopting it. Some **breeds*** of dogs were **bred*** to fight other dogs. They can be dangerous around children.

People might buy a puppy from a **breeder***. **Pure bred*** dogs may cost $500 to $3,000 or more. Breeders want to be sure that their puppies go to good "forever homes." Puppies in a pet store may be from mother dogs that did not have good care or **nutrition***.

Manners around dogs

Dog owners must make sure their dogs do not hurt or disturb others. Some dogs are not friendly to strangers. If you want to pet someone's dog, ask first, "May I pet your dog?"

Some dogs work as **service animals***. They **guide*** blind people or keep health watch for people with an illness. Please don't pet service dogs while they are working.

Let's talk about it.

1. What types of pets do Americans have?

2. What kinds of pets do people keep in your home country?

3. What pet do you have or would you like to have? Tell about it.

4. What are some things that a dog needs?

5. What are some things that a cat needs?

6. What are rabies shots? Why do dogs need them?

7. What makes a dog a "good citizen?"

8. What is an animal shelter? Why do some people give up their pets?

Using new words:

Match the word with its meaning.

_____ 9. to leave without caring for something

_____ 10. the nails on a cat's or dog's paws

_____ 11. to bother someone; to be a nuisance

_____ 12. a small animal kept as a pet in a cage

_____ 13. to kill with humane procedures

_____ 14. a deadly disease spread by an animal bite

A. hamster

B. rabies

C. put down

D. disturb

E. claws

F. abandon

Write a word in each sentence to make it correct. Choose from this list:
breed   litter box   bark   obedience   fine   pooper scooper

15. A cat can "do its business" in a _____.

16. A person might choose a certain _____ of dog.

17. Many dogs will _____ when a stranger comes to the door.

18. Dog owners may have to pay a _____ if they do not clean up after their dog.

19. Use a _____ to clean up after a dog "does its business" outdoors.

20. A dog and its owner can learn good manners in _____ classes.

Answers to Quizzes

1. Birthdays p 6

7. D
8. B
9. E
10. C
11. A
12. spanking
13. yell
14. secret
15. saint's
16. candles

2. Special Ages p 10

5. D
6. E
7. C
8. F
9. B
10. A
11. preschool
12. learner's permit
13. Selective Service
14. anniversary

3. Birth Signs and Birthstones p 14

10. D
11. E
12. A
13. F
14. B
15. C

16. G
17. ambitious
18. precious
19. bull
20. astrology

4. Schools in the United States p 18

10. C
11. B
12. E
13. D
14. A
15. F
16. board
17. impaired
18. research
19. standards
20. conference

5. Tips for Success in School p 22

9. E
10. F
11. A
12. G
13. D
14. C
15. B
16. electronic
17. heading
18. media center
19. requirements
20. assignment

6. Bullying in Schools p 26

7. B
8. E
9. A
10. C
11. D
12. anonymous
13. principal
14. reward
15. compassion
16. damage

7. High School Graduation p 30

8. C
9. E
10. B
11. A
12. D
13. economics
14. inspire
15. patriotic
16. requirements

8. Higher Education p 34

10. B
11. F
12. C
13. A
14. E

Answers to Quizzes

Higher Education, continued

15. D
16. apply
17. investigate
18. require
19. promoted
20. scams

9. Paying for College p 38

9. C
10. A
11. B
12. F
13. E
14. D
15. support
16. Grants
17. major
18. debt
19. income
20. excellence

10. Friendship in the United States p 42

9. C
10. D
11. E
12. F
13. B
14. A
15. peer pressure
16. wise
17. volunteer
18. buddies
19. adjust

11. Gender in the United States p 46

11. A
12. C
13. D
14. E
15. B
16. occupations
17. chores
18. breadwinner
19. gender

12. Love and Romance p 50

8. B
9. C
10. D
11. E
12. commitment
13. chaperone
14. curfew
15. risk
16. blind date

13. Getting Engaged p 54

9. B
10. D
11. A
12. C
13. bachelor
14. menu
15. traditional
16. celebrate
17. formal

14. A Traditional Wedding p 58

7. A
8. F
9. C
10. D
11. B
12. E
13. vows
14. congratulate
15. bridesmaids
16. master of ceremonies

15. A Wedding Guest p 62

7. D
8. C
9. B
10. E
11. A
12. attend
13. register
14. initials
15. decorate
16. appetizers

Answers to Quizzes

16. Having a Baby in the United States p 66

10. B
11. D
12. A
13. E
14. C
15. midwife
16. umbilical cord
17. maternity
18. procedure
19. Caesarian

18. Taking Care of Children in the United States p 74

9. B
10. D
11. C
12. A
13. F
14. E
15. childproof
16. secure
17. epidemic
18. time out
19. suitable

20. Family Pets p 82

9. F
10. E
11. D
12. A
13. C
14. B
15. litter box
16. breed
17. bark
18. fine
19. pooper scooper
20. obedience

17. Other Ways to Become a Parent p 70

7. D
8. A
9. B
10. E
11. C
12. agency
13. disabilities
14. Adoption
15. adoptee
16. right

19. Keeping Children Safe p 78

10. D
11. E
12. B
13. A
14. C
15. protect
16. pretend
17. kidnapped
18. abuse
19. booster seat

Glossary

Some of the words in the glossary have many meanings.
We give only the meanings that you need for this book.

4-H Club *noun phrase*. A club for learning farm skills and animal care.

abandon *verb*. To leave without taking care of someone or something.

ability *noun*. A skill.

abortion *noun*. Ending a pregnancy.

abstinence *noun*. Staying completely away from an activity or substance.

abuse *verb*. To harm a person.

accept *verb*. 1. To receive willingly. 2. To tolerate and allow to be. 3. To offer admission to an organiztion.

access *verb*. To get connected to; to be able to get something from.

accredited *adjective*. (A school) meets the standards of the state.

ACT *noun*. A test for college admission or placement.

addictive *adjective*. Can cause a person to become dependent on having a substance.

adjust *verb*. To start to understand how to live in a new place.

adolescent *noun*. A person who is between childhood and adult.

adopt *verb*. To take a child (or a pet) into one's family as one's own.

adoptee *noun*. An adopted child.

advanced placement *noun phrase*. Difficult classes in high school that may give college credit.

advice *noun*. Suggestions for doing something.

agency *noun*. A part of an organization that has a special function.

aide *noun*. A helper in a school, hospital, library, home, etc.

allergy *noun*. A sensitivity to food or a chemical that gives a person a bad reaction.

allow *verb*. To give a person permission to do something. To let.

altar *noun*. A table in a church or synagogue for religious purposes.

AMBER Alert *noun phrase*. A notice about a missing child.

anesthesiologist [AE nihs THEE zee AH loh jist] *noun*. A medical doctor with a specialty in reducing pain.

animal shelter *noun phrase*. A place that cares for animals that have been abandoned by owners.

anniversary *noun*. The day that something happened in the past.

anonymous [uh NAHN ih mihs] *adjective*. Without anyone knowing a person's name.

anthropology *noun*. The study of people in different societies.

anxiety *noun*. A worry that something bad is going to happen.

appetizer *noun*. A small snack before a meal.

applicant *noun*. A person who has applied or asked for a job, a scholarship, or entrance into a school.

apply *verb*. To ask for something such as a job or entry to a school.

appreciation *noun*. A showing of gratitude. Thankfulness.

apprenticeship *noun*. Learning a job by working for an expert in the job.

archer *noun*. A hunter with a bow and arrows.

argue *verb*. To disagree in an angry way.

Armed Services *noun phrase, plural*. The military: Army, Navy, Marines, Air Force, Coast Guard.

arrange *verb*. To cause a meeting to happen. To put into an orderly condition.

arrest *verb*. To take into custody by the police.

ashamed *adjective*. To feel bad about one's appearance, clothing, home, or some action one has done.

assembly *noun*. A large gathering of people.

assign [uh SIYN] *verb*. To give someone a job to do.

assignment *noun*. School homework.

astrology *noun*. The study of the effects of stars and planets on a person's life.

astrologer [uh STRAH luh jer] *noun*. A person who has studied how constellations and planets affect one's life and future.

athletic *adjective*. Good at sports.

athletics *noun, plural*. Sports.

attend *verb*. To go to a school, church, or event and participate in it.

attraction *noun*. The feeling of wanting to be with a person.

audience *noun*. A group of people who are watching an event.

auditorium *noun*. A large room where many people can watch an event or listen to music or speeches.

autism [AW tiz'm] *noun*. A condition in which a person does not develop normal social skills.

autograph *noun*. A person's written signature.

available *adjective*. Open to agreement; not otherwise busy.

average *adjective*. Normal; the most likely number; near the middle.

avoid *verb*. To stay away from.

baby bump *noun phrase, slang*. The beginning of the expansion of a pregnant woman's abdomen.

baby shower *noun phrase*. A party with gifts for a baby-to-be.

bachelor *noun*. An unmarried man.

bachelor's degree *noun phrase*. A college degree after four years; Bachelor of Science or Arts.

bachelorette [bæch luh REHT] *noun, slang*. A woman who has not been married.

bachelor party *noun phrase*. A party for the groom the night before he gets married.

background *noun*. Information about a person's family, work history, education, arrest record, etc.

bark *verb*. A dog's speaking voice.

based on *verb phrase*. A foundation to make decisions about.

behavior *noun*. The sum of a person's actions, good or bad.

benefits (friends with) *noun phrase*. Friends who have sex together.

best man *noun phrase*. A friend who assists a groom at his wedding.

bilingual *adjective*. Able to speak or give information in two languages.

biological (parent) *adjective*. One's actual parent, not an adopted parent.

birdseed *noun*. Seeds that birds eat.

birth certificate *noun phrase*. An official document that shows a baby's time and place of birth, with names of parents and doctor.

birth coach *noun phrase.* A person who helps a woman during the delivery of her baby.

birth sign *noun phrase.* One of the 12 signs of the zodiac for the month a person was born.

birthstone *noun.* A precious stone associated with a particular month.

blind date *noun phrase, idiom.* A date arranged by friends for two people who have never met before.

blood type *noun phrase.* A characteristic of blood, such as types A, B, AB, and O.

blue-collar *adjective, idiom.* Said of jobs for people who work with their hands.

board *noun.* 1. Group of people who make decisions for an organization. 2. Daily meals paid for by the semester. 3. A flat piece of wood.

board of education *noun phrase.* The group of people who manage a school district, hire teachers, etc.

body piercing *noun phrase.* Putting ornaments on one's body such as earrings, nose rings, eyebrow studs.

booster seat *noun phrase.* A raised seat with safety belts for a child.

borrow *verb.* To use something that you must return to the owner.

bouquet [boo KAY] *noun.* A pretty bunch of flowers to carry.

breadwinner *noun, idiom.* The person who works for money to pay for food, rent, and expenses.

breast-feed *verb.* To give milk to a baby from one's breasts naturally.

bred *past form of verb* **breed.** To select parent dogs for puppies.

breed *noun.* A type of dog such as collie, poodle, boxer, etc.

breeder *noun.* A person who raises and sells pure-bred dogs.

bride *noun.* A woman as she is getting married, and a short time thereafter.

bridesmaid *noun.* A woman who assists the bride.

Brownies *noun.* A club for girls 8 to 11; they learn games, crafts, and art.

bruise *noun.* A mark on a persons body from an injury.

buddy *noun.* A good friend.

budget *noun.* A plan for earning,

spending, and saving money.

buffet [buh FAY] *noun.* A table with many types of food; a person can choose the food and serve him or herself.

bull *noun.* A male bovine. (The female is a cow.)

bullying *noun.* The act of harming a smaller, younger, or less able person by a person or group of people.

buttocks [BUHT uhks] *noun.* The soft, fleshy muscles that you sit on; the "behind."

bystander *noun.* A person who sees something that is happening but is not taking part in the action.

cabinet making *noun phrase.* The skill of making kitchen closets.

Caesarian delivery *noun phrase.* Cutting the uterus to remove a baby.

calculator *noun.* A device to make it easy to work with numbers.

calmly [KAHM lee] *adverb.* Quietly.

caption *noun.* The description for a photograph or illustration.

career *noun.* A profession or a job for one's life work.

career development *noun phrase.* A class to teach young people about how to prepare for a career.

catering [KAY tuhr ing] **hall** *noun phrase.* A place with large rooms for parties.

celebrate *verb.* To have a good time to mark a happy occasion.

centenarian *noun.* A person who is one hundred years old.

ceremony *noun.* Formal activities at a wedding, funeral, or holiday.

champagne [shaem PAYN] *noun.* A type of bubbly wine for celebrations.

chapter *noun.* A part of a book.

character *noun.* 1. The personality and behavior of a person. 2. A person in a story, movie, or book.

characteristics *noun, plural.* Things about a person or object that you can describe: color, size, strength, intelligence, skills, age, etc.

chart *noun.* A way to show information visually (numbers, growth, changes, comparisons, etc.).

charter school *noun phrase.* A public school that has its own set of rules and goals.

chat *noun.* A short talk.

cherish *verb.* To love and care for.

chew *verb.* To use one's teeth.

child molester *noun phrase.* A person who has sexual contact with a child.

childproof *verb.* To make a place safe for a child.

child welfare agency *noun phrase.* A government group that enforces laws about the care of children.

choir [KWIY'r] *noun.* A group of singers in a church.

choking hazard *noun phrase.* A small object that a young child might put into his or her mouth.

chorus [KAWR ihs] *noun.* A group of singers.

claw *noun.* A cat's sharp nail.

club *noun.* A group of people who are interested in doing things together.

combination *noun.* The joining of two or more things together.

come out of the closet *verb phrase, slang idiom.* To tell others that one is homosexual (gay or lesbian).

comment *verb.* To say something.

commercial *noun.* An advertisement on radio or TV.

commit *verb.* 1. To do some activity. 2. To make a firm promise.

commit suicide *verb phrase.* To kill oneself.

commitment *noun.* A strong promise to be loyal to someone or to support some idea.

common *adjective.* 1. Usual; frequently occuring. 2. Having similar characteristics as another.

community college *noun phrase.* A small college that is partly supported by taxpayers in a city or county.

commute [kuh MYOOT] *verb.* To travel daily to work or school.

compassion *noun.* A feeling of sympathy for others, and treating others kindly.

complicated *adjective.* Having many parts; confusing.

compliment *noun.* An expression that praises a person. "You did a great job."

complimentary *adjective.* Pleasant words to praise a person.

conceive *verb.* To become pregnant.

concept *noun.* An idea.

conference *noun.* A meeting to give and get information.

confetti *noun.* Tiny pieces of colored paper that people toss in the air.

confirm *verb.* To say that a possible fact is actually true.

congratulate *verb.* To praise a person for an accomplishment;.

consent 1. *verb.* To give permission to someone. 2. *noun.* Agreement to allow something to happen.

constantly *adverb.* Without stopping.

constellation *noun.* A group of stars that form a picture in the sky.

consult *verb.* To get advice from a person who knows a particular subject.

contagious *adjective.* Can be spread from one person to another like a disease.

contraception *noun.* Devices or practices to prevent pregnancy.

contract 1. *noun.* A legal document telling the obligations between two people. 2. *verb.* To make smaller.

contractions *noun, plural.* The rhythmic pressure of muscles in a woman's uterus to push out a baby.

contribute *verb.* To give something to a person or group that needs it.

control *verb.* 1. To have authority over something; to make rules for.

cooperative learning *noun phrase.* Students working together in groups to do a project or solve a problem.

counseling *noun.* The act of giving suggestions or advice to someone.

couple *noun.* Two people; husband and wife.

crab *noun.* A water animal with a hard shell and two large claws.

create [kree AYT] *verb.* To make something that didn't exist before.

creative *adjective.* Good at making art, music, stories, or inventions.

credit *noun.* At a school, a point toward earning a diploma based on completing a course or exam.

crib *noun.* A safe bed for a baby.

crime *noun.* An act that breaks the law: robbery, murder, selling drugs.

criminal record *noun phrase.* A list of a person's convictions for crimes.

crossing guard *noun phrase.* A person who helps children cross a street safely on their way to school.

crush *noun, slang.* A strong liking for someone who is not attainable.

Cub Scouts *noun phrase.* Junior Boy Scouts for ages 8 to 11.

curfew [KEHR fyoo] *noun.* The time by when a person must be home.

curious *adjective.* Wanting to know many things.

current *adjective.* Happening now.

custodian *noun.* A person who takes care of and cleans a building.

custom *noun.* An action that has been going on for a long time.

customary *adjective.* In the way that things are done by most people.

cut off *adjective phrase.* A limit. A cut off age is the oldest that one can be to qualify for public high school.

cyberbullying *noun.* Harming a person by insults and false stories on Facebook and other social media.

damage *verb.* To harm, or destroy property or a person's reputation.

date *verb.* To meet for an activity and to get to know someone better.

dating scene *noun phrase.* Meeting people, looking for a good partner.

dating site *noun phrase.* An Internet website on which people can search for someone they'd like to meet.

debt [DEHT] *noun.* An amount of money that a person owes.

decade *noun.* A period of ten years.

decorate *verb.* To add things to make something more beautiful.

defecate [DEH fuh kayt] *verb.* To pass waste matter from the rectum.

delivery *noun* The time when a baby is being born.

demand 1. *verb.* To ask for something in a very insistent way. 2. *noun.* An urgent need.

depend *verb.* To be based on.

deserve *verb.* To merit; to do something that should have a reward.

details *noun, plural.* The facts about an event, person, story, etc.

device *noun.* A small machine or tool to do a job.

diabetes *noun.* A serious disease; too much sugar in the blood.

diaper *noun.* A baby's pants that can be changed when wet or soiled.

diploma *noun.* A document that shows that a person has completed a course of study at a school.

disability *noun.* The loss of a person's ability to see, hear, speak, walk, understand, etc.

discipline *noun.* Teaching of manners, behavior, etc.

discount *noun.* A special low price.

discriminate *verb.* To treat a group of people differently from another.

discrimination *noun.* The unfair treatment of a group of people.

discussion *noun.* A talking about a topic; sharing ideas about it.

disobey *verb.* To do something that is against a parent's rule or a law.

disturb *verb.* To annoy, irritate; to keep others from doing their work.

DJ (disc jockey) *noun.* A person who puts together musical selections to play at a party.

does his business *verb phrase, idiom euphemism.* Defecates or urinates.

doubt *verb.* To not believe something that is said or written.

draft *verb.* To take men into the Armed Services. 2. To make a drawing or write down the first ideas for a document or story.

drop out *verb phrase, idiom.* To leave school before graduating.

earn a living *verb phrase.* To work to make money to pay expenses.

economics *noun, plural.* The study of the ways money moves around, and how people use money.

effort *noun.* The work or energy that a person puts into a job.

elderly *adjective.* Old (a polite term).

elective *noun.* A subject that a student chooses to take.

electronic *adjective.* Using electricity and computers to operate.

embarrass *verb.* To make a person feel ashamed or bad.

emergency *noun.* A situation where people must act quickly.

employer *noun.* A person who gives a job to another person.

energetic *adjective.* Full of energy.

engage *verb.* To promise to marry.

epidemic *noun.* A condition or disease that affects many people.

escort [ehs KORT] *verb.* To guide a person by taking their hand or arm.

ESL = English as a Second Language.

ethnic *adjective.* Of a particular national group or culture.

euthanize [YOO thuh NIYZ] *verb.* To end an animal's life in a gentle way.

evaluate *verb.* To judge the worth of something.

excellence *noun.* A state of being very good; close to perfection.

exchange *verb.* To give a gift and receive a gift.

expect *verb.* To know that something will happen; to want something to happen in the future.

expectant mother *noun phrase*. A woman who is pregnant.

expel *verb*. To remove a student from a school for bad behavior.

expert *noun*. A person who knows a lot about a topic or is very skillful in an activity.

exploited *adjective*. Used badly; used for another person's benefit, harming the exploited person.

extra-curricular activities *noun phrase, plural*. Activities at school that are outside of classes: sports, clubs, cheerleading, service clubs.

Facebook *noun*. A free social media website on the Internet. It allows members to post photos and news for friends and others to see.

facilities *noun, plural*. Rooms, kitchen, bathrooms, buildings, etc. for an activity or organization.

FAFSA *noun*. Free Application for Federal Student Aid. A document for a student's family to give information about their earnings and savings.

federal *adjective*. National. A government over many states.

fee *noun*. A service cost.

fiancé [FEE ahn SAY] *noun*. A man who is engaged.

fiancée [FEE ahn SAY] *noun* A woman who is engaged.

file *verb*. To put a document in a correct place; to register a deed or license with the government.

financial aid *noun phrase*. Money that a student gets to help pay for the cost of higher education.

fine *noun*. A punishment in which one has to pay an amount of money.

form *noun*. A document that a person can fill in with information.

formal *adjective*. Following rules of convention or tradition; suitable for an important event or occasion.

foster parents *noun phrase, plural*. Parents who get government pay to provide a home and care for a child.

frame *verb*. To put a picture or document into a wooden structure so it can hang on a wall.

frank *adjective*. Blunt, honest, not holding back the truth.

frown upon *verb phrase, idiom.* To feel that some action is bad.

garter *noun*. A pretty elastic band worn by a bride on the upper leg.

gay *adjective*. Homosexual.

gem *noun*. A precious stone.

gender *noun*. Sex; male or female or transitional.

geography *noun*. The study of the world; maps, resources, capitals, etc.

genitals *noun plural*. Sex organs.

gerbil *noun*. A small rodent.

gluten [GLOO tihn]*noun*. A food element in wheat, rye, or barley flour. Some people become ill from eating food with gluten.

going steady *verb phrase, idiom*. Dating a person exclusively, without dating others.

Google 1. *noun*. The brand name of an Internet search engine. 2. *verb*. To look for information on the Internet.

gown *noun*. 1. A long, beautiful dress for a special occasion. 2.A robe over the clothing at graduation.

grade *noun*. 1. A level in school: first, second grade, for example. 2. A number or letter mark on a report card telling a student's achievement in school.

graduation *noun*. The ceremony upon completing a course of study.

grant *noun*. Money from government or college to help a low-income student pay for college costs.

groom *noun*. A man who is getting married.

ground *verb*. To keep a child at home after school as a punishment.

guest *noun*. A person who is invited to a party or wedding.

guidance counselor *noun phrase*. A professional who advises students about careers, job, or college, etc.

guide *noun*. 1. Someone who shows a person how go somewhere. 2. A book explaining rules and customs.

gynecologist [GIY nuh KAHL uh jist] *noun*. A doctor who treats women's medical problems.

hamster *noun*. A small rodent.

hang out *verb phrase, idiom*. To spend time with someone.

harm *verb*. To hurt.

have an edge *verb phrase idiom*. To be more able to achieve something.

heading *noun*. A title for part of a chapter.

headline *noun*. A news story title.

Headstart *noun*. School for children aged 3 to 5 in low-income neighborhoods.

high-income *adjective*. Earning more than $100,000 per year.

high-pressure *adjective*. Forceful, aggressive selling methods.

hire *verb*. To give a person a job.

hobby *noun*. An activity that a person does for fun, not for pay.

hold your applause *verb phrase*. Don't clap your hands yet.

homemaker *noun*. A person who takes care of a house and family.

homosexuality *noun*. Attraction to members of one's own sex.

honeymoon *noun*. A vacation for a just-married couple.

honor 1. *verb*. To show respect and appreciation for someone. 2. *noun*. A showing of great respect.

hormones *noun, plural*. Body chemicals that control emotions, hunger, parenting, fear, anger, sexual attraction, etc.

horoscope *noun*. A prediction based on a person's birth sign.

housebreak *verb*. To teach a dog to poop and pee outside the house.

identify with *verb phrase*. To feel that one is a certain gender.

immigrant *adjective*. A person who comes into a country to live.

impaired *adjective*. Unable to function normally; damaged.

improve *verb*. To make better.

income *noun*. Money a person gets from work, interest, pension, etc.

in common *adverbial phrase*. With similar ideas, interests, or characteristics as another person.

increase *verb*. To grow larger.

industry *noun*. The businesses that produce things; factories.

infant *noun*. A baby under one year.

inferiority *noun*. A sense of being not as good as other people.

informal *adjective*. Not full of rules.

inherited *adjective*. Gotten from one's parents.

initials *noun, plural*. Beginning letters of names or words.

inspect *verb*. To look at carefully.

inspire *verb*. To give ideas and energy to a person to do great things.

Instagram *noun*. Communication by Internet.

insult *verb*. To say things to hurt.

intercourse *noun*. Sexual union between male and female.

interview *verb*. To speak with a person to give and get information.
introduce *verb*. To help a person meet someone or something new.
invest *verb*. To give time or money in order to get more back later.
investigate *verb*. To get more information; to get answers to questions.
investment *noun*. Money or time a person spends to get an education or build a business.
iPad *noun*. A small computer.
justice of the peace *noun phrase*. A town official who performs marriages and keeps records.
kidnap *verb*. To steal a child.
kindergarten *noun*. A class before first grade, for 5-year-old children.
label *noun*. A tag or paper to tell what is inside of a container.
labor *noun*. The contractions of the uterus to push a baby out.
landlord *noun*. A person who rents an apartment or house to others.
laptop *noun*. A portable computer.
legal *adjective*. According to law; allowed by the law.
legal drinking age *noun phrase*. The age that a person may buy or drink alcoholic beverages.
lesbian [LEHZ bee'hn] *noun*. A girl or woman homosexual.
liberal arts *noun phrase, plural*. College courses in languages, history, literature, psychology, sociology, etc.
license *noun*. An official permit to own a dog, drive a car, marry, do a job etc.
limit *verb*. To set an outer extent for an amount of money, people, time, etc. 2. *noun*. That extent.
literature *noun*. Prose and poetry; stories, novels, and poems.
litter box *noun phrase*. A cat's toilet.
loan *noun*. Money that a person has borrowed.
local *adjective*. In one's own city, town, or neighborhood.
location *noun*. A specific place.
locker room *noun phrase*. The room where sports players change their clothes, shower, and dress.
lonely *adjective*. Feeling sad about being alone.
long-term *adjective*. For a long period of time.
lottery *noun*. An event in which winners are chosen by chance.

loyal *adjective*. True to a person or country; faithful.
maid of honor *noun phrase*. An unmarried woman who assists the bride.
major *adjective*. 1. Larger, most important. 2. *noun*. The group of classes that a student specializes in at a university. 3. *verb*. To take courses connected with a special field: Joe *majored* in chemistry.
make a fuss over *verb phrase, idiom*. To call attention to, and want others to think that an event or object is important.
make fun of *idiom*. To laugh at a person and cause others to laugh.
marking period *noun phrase*. A period of time during which teachers evaluate students' work for grades on a report card.
masonry *noun*. Stone work.
master of ceremonies *noun phrase*. A person who introduces speakers and events at a formal gathering.
maternity clothes *noun phrase, plural*. Clothes for a pregnant woman.
matron of honor *noun phrase*. A married woman who assists the bride.
mature *adjective*. Older, wiser; able to make good decisions.
maximum *adjective*. Upper limit; most.
mechanic *noun*. A person who can repair cars, machinery, etc.
media center *noun phrase*. A library with books, DVDs, CDs, computers, movies, and magazines.
media specialist *noun phrase*. A teacher in charge of the media center; a librarian.
medical technology *noun phrase*. Devices that help doctors diagnose, treat, and monitor a patient's condition.
memorize *verb*. To learn very well so it won't be forgotten.
menu [MEHN yoo] *noun*. A list of foods that a restaurant can serve.
mess *noun*. Something that is mixed up, out of place, or hard to fix.
midwife *noun*. A person who takes care of a woman during childbirth.
minimum *noun/adjective*. The least possible amount; the smallest.
minister *noun*. A leader of a congregation of a church.

minor *noun*. A person under age 18.
mobile *noun*. A visual toy hanging over a baby's crib or carriage.
moral *adjective*. Concerned with values of respect for others, for life.
mortarboard *noun*. A flat "cap" with a tassel hanging from one side.
mosque [mahsk] *noun*. A Muslim house of worship.
murder *verb*. The crime of killing a person in an unlawful manner.
nanny *noun*. A person who lives with a family to care for children.
nationality *noun*. The *adjective* for a country: Italy = *Italian*.
native language *noun phrase*. The language that a person learned in the first few years of life.
natural childbirth *noun phrase*. A system of giving birth without having any pain killers or anesthesia.
neglect *noun*. A lack of proper care for children or animals.
neuter [NOO tehr] *verb*. To remove the ovaries or testes of an animal.
newborn *adjective*. Brand new baby.
nifty *adjective*. Fine; stylish.
nightmare *noun*. A very bad dream.
nominate *verb*. To name a person to a job or important position.
nonagenarian [NOHN uh juhn AR ee uhn] *noun*. A person aged 90 to 99.
non-edible *adjective*. Not for eating.
novel [NAH v'l] *noun*. A book of fiction that tells a long story.
nutrition *noun*. The science of food and how it affects one's body.
obedience class *noun phrase*. A class where dogs learn good manners.
obstetrician [AHB stuh TRISH 'n] *noun*. A medical doctor who cares for pregnant women and delivers babies.
occasion *noun*. An event; a time that something happened.
occupation *noun*. A life long job or career.
Occupational Outlook (Handbook) *noun*. A large book that describes the future needs for different kinds of jobs, what salaries are, plus the training and skills needed.
octogenarian [AHK tuh jehn AR ee uhn] *noun*. A person aged 80 to 89.
offer *verb*. To say that one will give.
offer a toast *verb phrase, idiom*. To make a short speech to praise

a person or a couple at a wedding (followed by everyone drinking a small glass of champagne).

official *noun.* A person in charge of an event, ceremony, business, etc.

on their own *adverbial phrase.* Not living at home anymore; working and paying one's own bills.

one-night stand *noun phrase, idiom, slang.* A sexual connection for one night only.

openly *adverb.* Without hiding secrets; letting others know the facts.

opinion *noun.* A personal feeling or idea about a matter.

opportunity *noun.* A chance for something to happen in the future.

orphan *noun.* A child with no parents.

overly *adverb.* Too much.

overpopulation *noun.* The condition of too many animals or people.

pain relief *noun phrase.* A medicine or practice that reduces pain.

paraprofessional *noun.* An aide; a person who assists a professional.

parochial [puh ROH kee uhl] *adjective.* Supported by a church.

participate *verb.* To take part in a discussion or activity.

participation *noun.* Taking part in group activities; speaking in classroom discussions.

path *noun.* A road or direction.

patriotic *adjective.* Showing love of one's country.

peer pressure *noun phrase.* The influence of a person's friends.

Pell Grant *noun phrase.* Money from the government to help a student pay for higher education.

pension *noun.* A monthly payment to a person who has retired.

perform *verb.* To act in a drama; to do a job.

permission *noun.* Consent for a person to do something.

permit 1. [PER miht] *noun.* A document that allows a person to do something. 2. [per MIHT] *verb.* To allow some action.

petal *noun.* A part of a flower.

philosophy *noun.* The study of ways of thinking and explaining the world.

physical handicap *noun phrase.* An inability to see, hear, walk, talk, etc.

physical science *noun phrase.*

Science of the earth: geology, chemistry, physics, astronomy.

Pinterest *noun.* An Internet site where people can post photos.

platonic *adjective.* Without having a sexual relationship; just friends.

play date *noun.* A meeting for children to get together to play.

plumbing *noun.* Repairs for the system of pipes, sinks, toilets, and bathtub in a house.

pluses and minuses *noun phrase, plural.* The good and the bad parts.

politician *noun.* A person who is, or wants to be, elected to office.

poop *noun/verb, children's word.* Excrement; solid waste material from the digestive system.

pooper scooper *noun phrase.* A device to pick up a dog's poop.

pose *verb.* To sit or stand for a photograph.

positive *adjective.* A yes answer to a blood test to confirm a question.

post *verb.* To put a message or photo onto a website on the Internet.

poster *noun.* A large picture.

potential *noun/adjective.* Having a chance to be something in the future.

precious stone *noun phraase.* A jewel; diamond, ruby, pearl, etc.

prefer *verb.* To like one thing better than another.

pregnant *adjective.* Carrying an unborn baby; expecting a baby.

prenatal *adjective.* Before a baby is born.

pre-nuptial *adjective.* An agreement before marriage.

pre-teen *noun.* A person aged 10, 11, or 12.

prevent *verb.* To stop something from happening.

priest *noun.* The person in charge of a Catholic or Episcopal church.

principal *noun.* The person who manages a school.

privilege *noun.* A special right such as a child's privilege to watch TV.

procedure *noun.* 1. The way in which a job is done. 2. A medical or surgical action.

profession *noun.* A job such as doctor, lawyer, teacher, engineer, etc.

professional *noun.* A person with an occupation such as teacher, doctor, dentist, lawyer, scientist, etc.

profit *noun.* The money a business

earns after paying all of its expenses.

progress *noun.* Growth in skills and knowledge; advancement.

project *noun.* A task to create something for others to see or use.

promote *verb.* To move a student to the next grade; to give a worker a job with more responsibilty.

pronounce *verb.* 1. To say the sounds in a word or sentence. 2. To speak with authority.

property *noun.* Things that a person owns, such as money, house, or car.

propose *verb.* To ask someone to get married.

protect *verb.* To save from danger.

psychologist *noun.* A professional who treats people for anxiety, neurosis, depression, compulsions, etc.

public *adjective* 1. Open to anyone. 2. Paid for by the government.

pulse *noun.* The feel of a person's heartbeat, as felt in one's wrist.

purebred *adjective.* Having both parents of the same breed.

put down *verb phrase, idiom, euphemism.* To kill in a gentle way when an animal is not able to live.

R.S.V. P. *Respondez s'il vous plait.* [ray POHN day seel voo PLAY] Please respond. *Are you coming? Let me know.*

rabbi [RAE biy] *noun.* A Jewish religious leader.

rabies shot *noun phrase.* A vaccination against a deadly disease spread by a bite by an infected animal.

raid *verb.* To go to a place to arrest anyone who is breaking the law.

ram *noun.* A male sheep.

rape *noun.* The crime of forced sexual intercourse.

rare *adjective.* Very uncommon. Not happening often.

rear *noun.* The back part of something.

reception *noun.* A party after a wedding.

recommend *verb.* To suggest.

record *noun.* 1. A list of accomplishments, crimes, good deeds, etc. 2. A document that contains information about birth, marriage, or a legal transaction.

reduce *verb.* To make smaller.

refuse *verb.* To say no to an offer or request.

register *verb.* 1. To put one's name

on an official list. 2. To make a list of gift suggestions at a store.

registered *adjective*. Having a list at a store of things wanted as gifts.

regret *verb*. To feel sorry for something that one has done.

rehearsal *noun*. A practice.

rehearse *verb*. To practice so everyone knows what to do.

relate *verb*. To interact with people; to have social skills.

relative *noun*. A person who is a member of the family.

remedial reading *noun phrase*. A class to help slow readers improve.

report *verb*. To tell.

report card *noun phrase*. A notice to parents about their child's progress in school subjects.

representative *noun*. A person who speaks for, and votes for, others.

require *verb*. 1. To need. 2. To say that someone must do something.

requirement *noun*. Something that is needed.

research skills *noun phrase, plural*. Ability to gain information from books, Internet, interviews, etc.

reserve *verb*. To hold a place or an item for a time for someone.

resident *noun*. A person who lives in a place.

respect *verb*. To treat a person with politeness and kindness.

restaurant chain *noun phrase*. A number of restaurants all owned by the same person or corporation.

retire *verb*. To stop working after a lifetime of work.

retirement *noun*. The state of not working after a lifetime of work.

review *verb*. To study again.

reward *verb*. To give a prize for doing something well.

riot *noun*. Loud, violent actions by a group of excited or angry people.

risk *verb*. To take a chance that something will have a good result,

romantic *adjective*. With thoughts of love, pleasures, attraction.

rough draft *noun phrase*. The first, not-quite finished writing of a story.

rude *adjective*. Not polite.

run *verb*. 1. To try to be elected 2. To cause a computer program do its work.

sacred [SAY krihd] *adjective*. Holy; special to God or a religion.

saint's day *noun phrase*. Each day of

the year in the Catholic calendar is the day for a particular saint. **salary** *noun*. The earnings in a year.

salutatorian [suh LOO tuh TAWR ee uhn] *noun*. A graduate with the second highest grade point average.

sane *noun*. Not crazy.

SAT Scholastic Aptitude Test *noun*. A test for entry into college.

satisfy *verb*. To give a person what he or she wants.

scales *noun*. Devices for measuring weight (a symbol of justice).

scam *noun*. A set of lies and a plan to get people's money.

scholarship *noun*. Money to help a person pay for educational costs.

scorpion *noun*. A poisonous creature, related to spiders.

scratching post *noun phrase*. A place where a cat can clean its claws.

scream *verb*. To yell very loudly.

seal *verb*. To close tightly; to close a legal record so no one can see it.

second-hand *adjective*. Already used.

secretary *noun*. An office assistant.

secure *adjective*. Safe, not in danger.

security guard *noun phrase*. A person who protects a store or building.

Selective Service *noun phrase*. A government agency that keeps a list of young men in the country who can be called in case of emergency or war.

self-confidence *noun*. A feeling of being capable and worthy.

semester *noun*. One half of a school year at college.

senator *noun*. A person elected to congress to help make laws.

senior citizen *noun phrase*. Older person.

sensitive *adjective*. Having ability to see, hear, feel, taste in a stronger way than others.

service animal *noun*. A dog or other animal that has been trained to help a disabled person.

sexual orientation *noun phrase*. Whether a person is attracted to the opposite sex or the same sex.

sexually-transmitted *adjective*. A disease that can be spread by sexual contact.

shock *verb*. To surprise someone as if with electricity.

shower *noun*. A party for giving gifts.

shred *verb*. To tear into very small

pieces.

silly *adjective*. Not sensible; foolish.

similar *adjective*. Having features or characteristics that are like those of someone or something else.

sin *noun*. An act that is against a religious law.

sincerely *adverb*. With true feelings.

single *adjective*. Not married.

skill *noun*. An ability.

skip *verb*. To leave something out.

sleepover *noun*. A visit to a friend's house that includes sleeping there.

snack *noun*. A small meal; sandwich, apple, juice.

social media *noun phrase*. Facebook, Twitter, Instagram, chat sites.

Social Security *noun phrase*. A government-managed insurance program for people who become disabled or who retire after age 66.

social skills *noun phrase, plural*. Abilities to get along with people, make friends, express themselves.

social work *noun phrase*. A category of work that includes counselors, therapists, child protection workers.

sociology *noun*. The study of how people live, interact, and relate in different societies.

soloist *noun*. A musician who plays or sings without others.

source *noun*. The place or person something or some information comes from.

spank *verb*. To hit a child on the buttocks with an open hand.

spanking *noun*.

spay *verb*. To do surgery to prevent a female animal from having babies.

spellcheck *noun*. A computer program that can correct spelling.

spread *verb*. 1. To infect (as a disease) other people. 2. To scatter (with flowers, for example).

stand up for *verb phrase, idiom*. To defend; to speak in behalf of.

standards *noun, plural*. Levels of excellence or requirements to meet.

STEM Science, Technology, Engineering, and Math.

stormy *adjective*. Having arguments about differences of opinions.

stranger *noun*. A person who is not known to you.

stripper *noun, slang*. A person who

slowly takes off his or her clothes.

stroller *noun.* A baby carriage.

student teacher *noun phrase.* A person who is learning to teach.

substitute *noun.* Something that is used in place of an original.

suburb *noun.* The area just outside a big city.

suffocate *verb.* To die from no air.

suitable *adjective.* Has the right qualities for a job or to be a good partner.

superstition *noun.* A belief that people used to regard as true.

support *verb.* To pay for a person's expenses.

surgeon *noun.* A doctor who cuts into bodies to repair it.

surgery *noun.* The cutting into a body to treat a disease or repair something that has broken.

surrogate *noun.* A person who does something for someone who cannot do it.

suspect *verb.* To think something might be true.

suspend *verb.* To require a student to leave school for several days.

sweets *noun, plural.* Candy, cookies, cake, pie, pudding, desserts, etc.

switch *verb.* To exchange one thing for another.

sympathetic *adjective.* Having similar feelings; a good match.

synagogue [SIN uh gahg] *noun.* A Jewish house of worship; a temple.

target *noun.* 1. A goal. 2. A person that a bully hurts.

taste buds *noun phrase, plural.* The tiny organs on the tongue that can sense the flavors in food.

tattoo *noun.* Words or pictures that are drawn with ink on skin.

tease *verb.* To make fun of in a playful way.

technical [TEHK nih k'l] *adjective.* With skills and techniques [tehk NEEKS] of certain occupations.

technology [tehk NAH loh jee] *noun.* Devices, computers, and machines to do work.

teen *noun.* A person aged 13 to 19.

temple *noun.* Jewish house of worship.

text 1. *noun.* Written words. 2. *verb.* To send a message on a cell phone.

threaten *verb.* To say that one is going to do something that will hurt.

tight budget *noun phrase, idiom.* Not enough money to spend.

time (to) *verb.* To take note of the time between contractions.

time out *noun phrase.* A gentle punishment: staying away from activities for several minutes.

tips *noun, plural.* Advice; suggestions for doing something. 2. Extra money given to a waiter, delivery person, taxi driver, etc.

toast *verb.* To speak words to honor a person at a special occasion.

Toastmasters *noun.* A club to help people learn public speaking.

toddler *noun.* A child from the time it begins to walk to about age 3.

topic *noun.* Something that a person writes about or talks about.

toss *verb.* To throw.

town clerk *noun phrase.* An official who keeps records for the town.

traditional *adjective.* Done in a way that has been done for a long time.

transcript *noun.* A document that lists classes and grades that a student has completed.

transfer *verb.* To move something from one place to another.

transgender *noun/adjective.* Having the body of a male, but the mind and brain of a female, or vice versa.

treat 1. *verb.* To pay for someone's dinner, ticket to the movies, etc. 2. To handle, speak to, manage. 3. *noun.* Something good, a reward, snack, cookie, dessert, etc.

Treat me with respect. *request.* Do not insult me or hurt me.

treatment *noun.* Medicine, surgery, advice for a sick person.

tuition *noun.* The cost of education.

tuxedo *noun.* A man's formal jacket.

twins *noun, plural.* Two babies born at the same time to a mother.

Twitter *noun.* Social media for sending very short messages (Tweets).

two-weeks' notice *noun phrase.* Telling an employer that one will be leaving a job in two weeks.

ultrasound *noun/adjective.* A procedure that uses sound to show things inside a person's body.

umbilical cord *noun phrase.* The cord leading from the placenta to the unborn baby.

unconstitutional *adjective.* Against the Constitution of the United States.

unkind *adjective.* Hurtful.

unsweetened *adjective.* Without sugar.

up to you *adverbial phrase.* 1. You get to choose. 2. It's your job or responsibility.

urge *verb.* To strongly advise.

urine [YOO rihn] *noun.* A body's waste water; pee.

usher *noun.* A person who shows someone the way to a seat.

vaccination *noun.* An injection of medicine to prevent a disease.

vague [VAYG] *adjective.* Not clear.

valedictorian *noun.* The person in a graduating class who has the highest grade point average.

vary *verb.* To be different at different times or in different places.

variety *noun.* A collection of different things.

veterinarian *noun.* A doctor for animals.

vice versa *adverb phrase.* The other way around; in the opposite direction.

vice principal *noun phrase.* An assistant principal.

victim *noun.* A person who has been hurt in an accident, or by bullying.

virgin [VUHR jihn] *noun.* A person who has never had sexual intercourse.

virginity *noun.* The condition of being a virgin.

vision *noun.* The ability to see; the hopes for a future.

vocabulary *noun.* The words that a person learns or knows.

vow *noun.* A serious promise.

water may break *verb phrase.* The fluid in the uterus may flow out.

wedding party *noun phrase.* The bride, groom, their parents, the bridesmaids, and ushers.

welding *noun.* The skill of melting metal to join other metals together.

well-rounded *adjective.* Having knowledge in many fields.

wise *adjective.* Able to make good decisions.

witness *noun.* 1.0 A person who has seen an event or an accident. 2. A person who sees a marriage ceremony and signs the license.

women's liberation movement *noun phrase.* Series of actions by many groups to change laws and customs regarding women and men.

yearbook *noun.* A book of photos and events for graduating students.

zodiac *noun.* The path of the sun in the sky, behind which are the unseen constellations.